Touching Grandma's Heart

Touching Grandma's Heart

ISBN #978-1-60920-066-4
Copyright ©2013 Connie L Hawkins.
All rights reserved.
Printed in the United States of America.

Library of Congress Cataloging-in-Publication Data

For more information or to contact the author write to:
Ajoyin Publishing PO Box 342, Three Rivers, MI 49093
Or email: authorconnielhawkins@yahoo.com

Touching Grandma's Heart

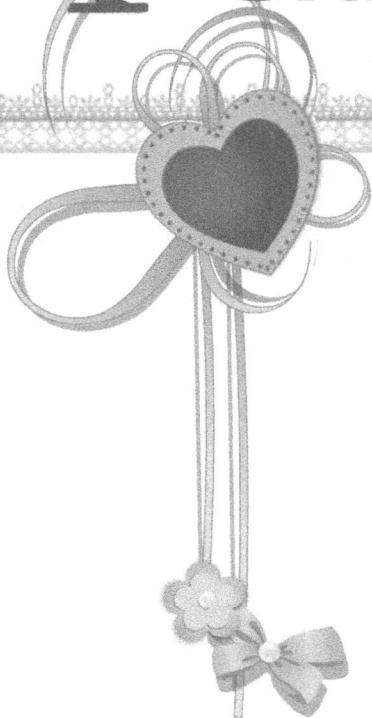

Connie L Hawkins

Ajoyin Publishing, Inc.
PO Box 342
Three Rivers, MI 49093
1.888.273.4JOY
www.ajoyin.com

Dedicated to first-time grandmas everywhere!
And to my adorable grandchildren.

A March Miracle

"Seeing, hearing, feeling, are miracles, and each part and tag of me is a miracle."
~Walt Whitman

March 30, 2009, I became a grandma for the first time. I was 63 years old. Most of my friends were working on great-grandchildren and here I was doing the first-time Grandma dance! I had waited a long time. As I looked down at the miracle of life before me, swaddled in innocence, I was moved by God's awesome creation. My heart filled with both joy and fear.

Joy because of the blessing that God had given me by allowing me to be here for the birth of my first grandchild; it is not a blessing I will ever take for granted and one that I will cherish for the rest of my days.

Father, (Great-Grandpa) mother, son and now a grandson—life had come full circle. I couldn't wait to teach this little one what I know to be true and wondered as I held him in my arms for the first time the lessons he would teach me.

"Together little man we will create a chain of love that links the past with the future." I whispered into his ear. He looked up I was sure he was smiling. I don't care what anyone says, I know he recognized my voice.

The fear came in knowing that this little bundle of pure joy and happiness comes into the world knowing nothing. Everything is still to be learned; life is yet to be experienced. Although it's a parent's job to teach, to mold and to shape, it's also a grandparent's responsibility. We bestow upon our grandchildren strength and wisdom that time and experience has given us. We pass that wisdom, if they will allow it, on to our grandchildren and we should not take our role lightly. We are family. I read somewhere … the chain may lengthen but it will never be broken. Welcome to the world Little J—short for Jeremiah Matthew.

As day one of the miracle of life turned into day two, three and four. I knew without doubt that I would probably write a book about life with Little J. The words were already forming in my head. How could they not— he was awesome, adorable—cute as button. Wait a minute; buttons aren't that cute are they? Cute for sure and definitely unique. Little J has no idea but within him lies the gift of many miracles.

"Hope... is the companion of power, and the mother of success; for whom so hopes, has within him the gift of miracles."
~Samuel Smiles

Inspiring

"Inspiration and genius—one and the same."
~Victor Hugo

I held Little J when he was just an hour old. Everything about him fascinated me. I could not take my eyes off him. It was as if this little one had cast a spell upon me. I think he did—it was guanine love.

Nine months thinking about this moment; I was so elated to finally meet this little man. But what inspired me even more and moved me to write the following poem was J's Papa, his mother's father, meeting this precious little one for the first time. Seeing the two of them together stirred the writer in me to pick up a pen that very day and put these words to paper.

Hello J. Matthew...
Papa's been waiting to meet you.
I have much in my heart to tell you.
Where should I start?
I'll be watching you grow
And teaching you things
I think you should know.
I'll help you plant flowers;
We'll play in the snow.
I can't wait for you to meet Jesus;
He's someone you'll want to know.
So happy to meet you I am...
By the way, J. Matthew, you're a Tiger's fan!
I'll teach you about baseball—all that I can.
We'll have such fun just wait and see!
You're Papa's boy, and you'll always be special to Jesus and me.
~Written by Connie Hawkins on March 30, 2009

I hope that Papa Place doesn't mind my sharing this piece of writing; the writing process has begun. The words are in my heart. I just have to put them on paper.

> "If you have built castles in the air, your work need not be lost; that is where they should be. Now put foundations under them."
> ~Henry David Thoreau

Awesome

"Our awesome responsibility to ourselves, to our children, and to
the future is to create ourselves in the image of goodness, because
the future depends on the nobility of our imaginings."
~Barbara Grizzuti Harrison

Joseph Joubert once said that "Imagination is the eye of the soul." As a
writer I believe that to be true. Sharing my life as an author with school
age children, instilling in them the awesomeness of imagination has been
a joy and now to think that I can share that same remarkable experience
with my own grandchild is beyond humbling—it is awe-inspiring. To
teach is to learn.

Every day that I visit Little J, I am amazed at what he's already learned.
Of course, I'm Grandma so everything this little man does from burping to
turning his head is extraordinary! Every grandma thinks her grandchild is
adorable, the most beautiful, most outstanding and super intelligent. There
is no doubt in my mind that my grandson is gifted—a genius if you will.

"Passion holds up the bottom of the universe and genius paints up
its roof."
~Chang Ch'ao

Genius is the capacity to see great things and find good in every relationship. J weighed in at 8 pounds 3 ounces, tiny but mighty. There is no un-
certainty in my mind that Little J is destined for great things. His steps
will be ordered by the Lord; his path made known by God. I don't know
much about the prophet Jeremiah *"but in private life he could have very
likely been a person of the most playful humor, brimful of fun and merriment."* ~Samuel Butler.

Although he's only a month old Jeremiah is truly awesome. He has
touched my heart, filling it with awe and with merriment; he makes me
laugh; he astounds me with his own form of creativity; he can melt your

heart in a minute, drag you into his moment to shine. Life has never been more delicious than it is as a grandma.

"I'm just working and having a good time and seeing what develops, which is so awesome, because you don't know what's going to happen, and I'm letting myself do that a lot more than I ever have."
~Kathleen Hanna

Incredible

"I can believe anything provided it is incredible."
~Oscar Wilde

The definition of incredible: Not credible; surpassing belief; too extraordinary and improbable to admit of belief; unlikely; marvelous; fabulous.

Extraordinary, marvelous and fabulous—that's how I would describe Little J. One of the things I find totally fascinating about babies is their unique ability to laugh at themselves and at every one else in their world. Wouldn't it be incredible if we could all laugh at ourselves like that? Or, if we would esteem everyone in the same way we highly esteem our little ones.

When I published my first book, *Sailing Through Life In A Rowboat*, I carried it around with me wherever I went, and I looked at it every day just to make sure that the ink hadn't faded. Now, I carry around pictures of Little J. Grandma's brag book, if you will. Every grandma should have one! If you're a grandma and don't have a "brag book," run out and get one this instance and fill it with a thousand pictures. These pictures are your memories.

Actually, (yes, I'm admitting it) I have three scrapbooks filled with pictures of this precious boy. I have a slide show, a power point presentation, and equal amounts of photo files on my computer; I look at them every day as a reminder of how incredible my grandson is and how incredibly blessed I am to be his grandma.

The first time he rolled over I applauded. "Look what you can do," I said. When he smiles at me I become putty in his hands and he knows it. When he's unhappy he comes to Grandma because he knows Grandma will fix it if she can.

Maybe some day, if I am lucky, Jeremiah will feel the same way about me and say, "My grandma is incredible; she's awesome." I can only hope.

"Incredibility is the wisdom of a fool" says Josh Billings or it could be the astonishing mind-blowing love of your grandchildren.

~Carl Sagan said, "Somewhere, something incredible is waiting to be known." Or someone, and that someone is none other than my grandson!

Boys and Their Toys

"As men get older, the toys get more expensive."
~Marvin Davis

The first thing I had to learn about being a "grandma" was an understanding of boys and their toys.

"A bee is never as busy as it seems, it's just that it can't buzz any slower," said Kin Hubbard. I like that analogy. J is a busy bee, perpetual motion in action. A boy on the go; noise in the disguise of a boy! He enjoys his toys. He likes taking them out of the toy box one by one and then putting them back into the toy box one by one.

And of course, he has his share of baby toys, rattles that make noise, rubber ducks that squeak, learning games and musical things, but he'd rather play with plastic lids! He enjoys opening and closing things, boxes, cell phones, doors and plays with any number of toys that might open and close, and, he really likes boxes. I bought him a small red (play) cell phone. Yes, it makes noise—it rings and has a dial tone but J doesn't care about any of that he just sits and opens and closes it. But the thing he really likes about the phone is that it's just like Grandma's phone! Ring … ring … it's for you!

He loves to play with hats, especially Grandpa's hat. It's an old camouflage hunting hat. He learned early on how to pull the hat off Grandpa's head then put it back on again. That was a favorite game from the get-go. Later, the new game was to throw the hat on the floor so Grandpa could turn him upside down and let him retrieve the hat. We've tried various hats, but the old hunting cap is the one. So, I bought J a hat just like Grandpa's for his first Christmas; now he has two hats he can put on and take off—what fun. He eventually outgrew the "hat" game and went on to more amusing games.

Grandpa's job is to give the little man rides on his fire truck. (It also makes noise). It's a tiring task but Grandpa's up to it. The squeals of sheer delight are worth the sore back. He can also stand and push it around the room, Little J that is, not Grandpa. We were so excited the first time he did it. "Amazing," is what his father said. Of course, he would get stuck and let out a bellowing scream whenever that would happen, which usually means, come get me … turn this thing around so I can go go go! And there he goes straight into the Christmas tree!

He is definitely a little man on the go, constantly moving, always something new to learn … how to push the dump truck around, building blocks and knocking them down. Opening and closing his toy computer, making music on his drum or reading his favorite bubble book. Grandma doesn't mind the games he's plays as long as it's OK that Grandma plays with him!

"What are little boys made of? Frogs and snails and puppy-dogs' tails, that's what little boys are made of."
~Nursery Rhyme

The Beauty of Being Grandma

"A grandmother is a little bit of parent, a little bit of teacher, and a little bit best friend."
~Author Unknown

I'm loving being a grandma. Little J is only 8 weeks old … and oh, the faces he can make. It didn't take him long at all to discover that whenever he made a funny face all the adults would laugh, coo and ah, and, he would feed right into that and make faces all the more; he has his own spiked hair doo going on, which makes him even more comical. What can I say, he's adorable. It's true, what the scholars say, "When a baby's born a grandma is made." This is what I have learned so far about being a grandma:

1. I've turned into my mother! I have wrinkles. I am now "Grandma."

2. It's wonderful to be a mom but it's even more wonderful to be a grandma, cuz they don't live with you 24/7!

3. Grandma's get to spoil and pamper. We can feed the little ones full of sugar and then send them home!

4. We can watch them spit up and smile about it.

5. We can listen to them make those little "grunting" noises and quickly hand them back to Daddy when it's time to change the diaper.

6. We don't have to worry about grouchy, fussy and teething. We just have to love. And hope that they will love us when we are grouchy, and fussy.

7. It only takes a moment when that little finger curls around yours for you to realize you are madly in love (again).

8. A new baby is a new beginning. It makes you realize the importance of past generations, the value of family history. You suddenly appreciate your own grandparents and the things you learned from them and you are anxious to past down those same stories to your grandchildren.

9. Having a new baby to think about makes you realize you aren't too old to dream and hope; suddenly you have dreams and hopes that hopefully you will get to share with your grandchildren.

10. I'm still learning the difference between a smile and gas—but I'm getting there.

Some grandmas will tell you that having grandchildren makes you feel young again. I think it depends on just how young a grandmother you are. I'm in my 60s and already realizing that spending more than an hour at a time with grandchildren quickly ages you. But at the same time I also realize that a home without a couple of grandma's in it isn't all that much fun. Little J is a lucky lad, he has Gamma Connie and his Nana and we are all going to have so much fun Carl Sandburg, one of my favorite poets, wrote that, "A baby is God's opinion that the world should go on." I truly believe it. I will enjoy this phase of my life—it's good to know that God's not done with me yet. I still have lots to do! I have grandchildren to love!

> If your baby is "beautiful and perfect, never cries or fusses, sleeps on schedule and burps on demand, an angel all the time, you're the grandma."
> ~Teresa Bloomingdale

Unconditional Love

"There is a miracle that happens every time to those who really love;
the more they give, the more they possess of that precious nourish-
ing love from which flowers and children have their strength and
which could help all human beings if they would take it without
doubting ..."

~Rainer Maria Rilke

You know what's great about grandchildren? They love unconditionally,
much like Christ loves us. No exceptions. They give you a smile and a hug
without any expectations. They run to the door and greet you with genuine
excitement. They will give you a bite of their cookie before you even ask.

They are innovative and creative in their efforts to achieve even the
most difficult of tasks just to please you and they never give up. They have
innocence about them that gives you hope when it comes to forgiveness,
laughter and the wonders of life.

To a child a flower is a miracle, laughter is necessary and dreams are
forever. They are accepting of life's conditions and with little effort learn
to endure adversity. They have a spirit of adventure about them and really
don't think much about time. To a child, time is not an issue. They have
all the time in the world.

Oh, the things that we could learn from children and grandchildren.

"Be not afraid of greatness: some are born great, some achieve greatness, and some have greatness thrust upon them."

~William Shakespeare

The Essence of Time

"God had infinite time to give us; but how did He give it? In one immense tract of a lazy millennium. No, but, he cut it up into a neat succession of new mornings, and with each, therefore, a new idea, new inventions, and new applications."
~Ralph Waldo Emerson

Surprisingly, God left these new ideas and new inventions into the hands of each new generation. There will come a time in J's life that he will pick up these ideas and run with them. Create new inventions of his own and maybe even figure out the essence of time that time itself is an element not to be taken lightly.

But when you are not even one, yet, time has no hold on you. It neither flies nor stands still—it just is. But for me time sure seems to fly by when you're having fun and I sure am having fun being grandma to my wonderful little imp of a grandson. I don't mind a bit sharing my time with him. In fact, I have all the time in the world to share.

The great thing about children is that they don't think about time. They don't think about the past, they don't worry about the future, they simply enjoy the present time, which few of us seem to do. Adults are always thinking about what we have to do tomorrow, or about the things we didn't get done today. There never seems to be enough time in a day to get things done—none of that matter's to children; time seems to stand still for them it has no bearing on their day. When they are hungry they eat. When they are tired they sleep. When they are happy they giggle. They have all the time they need to play and who better to play with them then Grandma and Grandpa, Nana and Papa; after all we have the same concept of time as our grandchildren.

The older I get I think the more I realize that time is a great innovator and there is nothing if left to time that cannot be worked out; there are no optical illusions in time or in its space; you can see more clearly over the space of time as you age and believe it or not you do have all the time you need in the world so use it wisely.

(This article first appeared in His Banner Newspaper and can also be viewed on Connie's Blog.)

"Time is the coin of your life. It is the only coin you have, and only you can determine how it will be spent. Be careful lest you let other people spend it for you."
~Carl Sandburg

The Laughter and the Fun

~Josh Billings once said, "Laughing is the sensation of feeling good all over, and showing it principally in one spot." And there is never one so good at showing that as a child.

It's true that kids say the "darnest" things, but they also do the cutest things. My father built my son a toy box when he was two. This box now belongs to the little man. As soon as he was walking, he figured out that if he turned the container that held his blocks upside down he could use it as a stool to stand on, making himself taller, therefore, making it easier to get into his toy box. Now is that genius or what? Of course, he has to throw everything out in order to find that very special toy in the bottom of the box. Soon he'll be asking, "Why is the favorite toy always at the bottom?"

J loves books—and of course he should. After all, his grandma is a writer! It's so much fun to watch him read to himself to hear him babbling. When he was a baby he loved the Sesame Street books, as a toddler he was into Bob the Builder and now that he's growing into a little boy he loves picture books that allow him to identify the objects. He gets pretty excited when he sees an elephant—not only does he know what it is he can make the sound—impressive.

He's learning to talk ... che is cheese. Muse ... could be milk, but I'm pretty sure it's music. One night at grandma's (J was spending the night) I was watching TV in my bedroom. J came in with his blanket and a book, turned off the TV and climbed up on my bed. "Muse," he said pointing at the TV. I had no idea what he was trying to tell me. After about twenty minutes of J screaming, "Muse" and pointing to the television, I put the TV channel on a music station. From that point on he was all smiles.

"She'll be coming 'round the mountain when she comes ..." causes J to break into fits of laughter, especially the line ... she'll have to sleep with Grandma when she comes ... "Sleeps with Gamma," he repeats in fits of laughter.

His play is busy work. In the kitchen he takes all the magnets off the frig and scatters them around the room before he picks them up and carefully reassembles them; he checks the dishwasher before coming over to the kitchen table for some one-on-one with play dough, coloring book and the crayons and later, as he got older—paints. Then it's down the hall to check out the bedroom. He comes back with Grandpa's collection of Match Box cars (J's now) and Grandma's lip gloss and tub pillow!

Next is the office. J loves to sit on Grandma's lap and watch Power Point slide shows starting the wonderful, exciting, and awesome Little J. We can actually spend a good hour in the office. But that reminds the little man that there's a digital picture frame in the living room also featuring the infamous J. He takes off in a mad dish; he thinks it's his own little TV. He pulls up his rocking chair or sits on the floor and watches himself on TV. He can indentify most of the people in the show!

"Ask not what fun does for you; ask rather what you do for fun."
~The Qaquia

Let There Be Music

"My music is best understood by children and animals."
~Igor Stravinsky (1882–1971)

Little J loves to play the "pano." He doesn't just bang on it; he actually positions his hands just so and in his mind begins to play a tune. He's been doing this for quite some time, since he was old enough to climb up on the piano. When his song is finished, he claps and looks to make be sure that we are clapping, too!

No one plays the piano quite like J plays the piano. "Yeah." We all clap.

As he grew older his piano playing got more intense.

I love it when he comes over, pulls out the piano bench, climbs up, opens the cover, turns to me and says, "Gamma, I think you would like a concert."

Does he know his Grandma well?

He plays loudly at first and then softly, using the black keys. "This is Gamma's song," he announces. "Wendell sleep," he commands the dog. "I play quiet."

When he's finished with his quiet music, we must clap quietly. But when he's not playing softly then he expects loud cheers and lots of admiration. "Gampa … you not clapping." He'll let you know if you fall short on your end.

One of J's favorite things to do at Grandma's house is Karaoke; he's quite the ham with a microphone in his hand. He's forever pestering Grandma about the Karaoke machine.

I tell him we can only play karaoke when the ladies are over, which reminds me of my Karaoke Night. Grandpa was deer hunting so I invited the girls over for a karaoke party. At the last minute I was asked to babysit for a couple of hours and wondered what I would do with Little J when the ladies arrived. No problem. He grabbed a microphone and joined right in. Every time someone performed Little J was there to clap. He was a one-boy audience and never missed a beat. What a groupie!

It's going to be a hot time in the ole town tonight … .we sang. "Yeah" J chimes. Everyone claps. What was I thinking? Little J is the Karaoke King!

When karaoke was finished we all adjourned to the living room for a private "pano" concert. Way to go Little J. Whether, singing, dancing or playing the "pano," the applause is never ending.

Now, when J wants Grandma to get out the karaoke machine I tell him we have to wait for the ladies. One day he grabbed the phone and said, "... ladies." He wanted me to call the girls; it was time for a karaoke party!

Yep, I'm already planning another karaoke night at the Hawkins house.

"Happiness does not consist in pastimes and amusements but in virtuous activities."

~Aristotle

Crying Over Spilled Milk

"It doesn't matter how much milk you spill, just so long as you don't lose the cow."

~Mark Guilbeau

Be prepared, with children comes an assortment of mishaps from broken toys to spilled milk, to arguments with siblings. It cannot be avoided—no matter what. "He is truly wise who gains wisdom from another's mishap." Publilius Syrus quotes (Roman author, 1st century B.C.)

One day at the little man's house, we had just finished lunch, J got down from his chair and accidently spilled his milk on the floor.

"Oh Oh." He ran to get a paper towel. Before he could get back the dog licked up the milk. Little J was so upset he sat down and cried.

I didn't know if I should spill some more milk so he could wipe it up or comfort him. Before I could make a decision J is scolding the dog and was quite serious about it. I bet the lesson learned that day had something to do with not crying over spilled milk!

One day at my house he was trying to climb up on the kitchen chair; it has rollers on it, so it's not an easy task when you are only two. The chair tipped over dumping the little man on the floor. "That chair bumped my head." He said. Then came tears followed by hugs.

It's not unusual to find a trail of water leading from the refrigerator to the table. J has learned how to go to the filtered pitcher of water and pour himself a cold drink—well, he has sort of learned. He just forgets to turn the water off.

One Christmas Heidi's dog, Dudley, grabbed a Christmas cookie out of Little J's hand. There was lots of screaming and yelling, especially when it happened a second time. J went tearing down the hallway to the office where Aunt Heidi and Daddy were working on Grandma's computer. He stood in the doorway screaming and yelling and pointing at Dudley.

"Jeremiah why are you screaming?" Aunt Heidi wanted to know. "Stop screaming and use your indoor voice."

"Time out Dudley," he sobbed.

If anyone does anything wrong they have to go to time out. We were driving J home one day when Grandpa came to a rolling stop, instead of a complete stop, at a country road intersection.

"Gampa ... didn't stop," J scolded. "You need time out."

"...and the Truth will Make you Laugh."
  ~The Oaquia

The Time Out Chair

~Cervantes said, "It is one thing to praise discipline, and another to submit to it."

The Bible says to spare the rod is to spoil the child. When I was a kid growing up there wasn't such a thing as a time out chair. We had to stand with our faces pressed into a corner. Whenever my kids would argue and/or call each other names, I'd make them sit in chairs facing one another; they had to give out compliments for 20 minutes. That must have seemed like an eternity to them.

One would think that someone as sweet and as talented as our little man that he wouldn't even know what a "time out chair" is. But that's not the case. There are days when J spends more time in the "time out chair" than he does any place else. Sometimes when Mother is punishing this child, Grandma has to leave the room not because I'm moved to tears but because I can't conceal my laughter.

In the beginning the time out chair was his dad's recliner. The minute Mom turned her back, the little man was up to no good … like making faces at his mother or climbing up on the back of the chair. The minute she'd turn around he'd scoot back unto his bottom with a very serious look on his face. Even when he was still a babe, he was up to no good. One time on the changing table he was wiggling and moving to the point where Mom began to count. She told him he needed to behave; she finally got the diaper on him and put him down on the floor. In retaliation he threw socks at her! (Grandma had to leave to the room.)

Later on the time out chair was the little white deck chair, usually he faces the wall but not without looking back at you, making faces and babbling. When he thinks no one's looking he gets up and runs around the room. It's right back to time out for another 3 minutes. Now time out is wherever (usually his room) and whenever Mom is frustrated with his antics.

Now why would such an adorable boy need time out? Let me count the ways: Splashing water out of the dog's dish or better yet eating the dog's food. (I've caught him several times down on all fours lapping water out of the dog's dish!)

Stuffing magnets into Daddy's VCR.

Tearing pages out of his books.

Squirting hand lotion all over himself, (and the dog if he can catch him) and sprinkling his room with baby powder. Dragging the kitchen chair over to the micro wave so he can open and close the door until he blows a fuse.

Standing on the kitchen table to dance is definitely a no no, but he's so cute.

Pulling the dog's tail always earns J some time in the time out chair.

Playing with Mom's jewelry or getting into her makeup—I definitely can see more time out in J's future.

And this is only the beginning—he's turning two!

"You can learn many things from children. How much patience you have, for instance."
~Franklin P. Jones

What's Not to Love About Being Outdoors?

"There is no other door to knowledge then the door nature opens."
~Luther Burbank

When J brings his coat and shoes to you it can only mean one thing—he wants to go outdoors. Backyards are a playground of adventure for this little man. Winter, spring, fall or summer, J can always find some source of amusement in the great outdoors. Whether he's in his own backyard space, or roaming Grandpa's two acres, or at the park; there is much to discover in nature and Little J is ready!

The sky, daily bread for our eyes. The earth—all that dirt. What's not to love?

A tree, beauty for some, an obstacle in your path for others. Fences to climb. Flowers to plant or to pluck. A dog to chase, and leaves to rake—or not!

Swings to swing on, horses to ride. A wild trip down the slide, deck chairs to rearrange. How 'bout a journey to the park in my little red wagon, Dad? We're going to the beach! Where are my goggles?

Water, wind and sand, rocks to collect and other buried treasures yet to be discovered.

Little J loves to come to Grandma's. He follows his grandpa everywhere and is particular mesmerized with Pa's pole barn. And why shouldn't he be? There's so much stuff to get into out there. And getting into "stuff" is what J does best. He loves to sit on Grandpa's tractors, especially the one that sits outside. I think he thinks Pa parked it there for his amusement. Before J could walk, Grandpa went out and bought a swing set for the backyard. J calls our backyard "the park." Also for his pleasure a dune buggy, an electric car and a Little John Deer tractor just like Grandpa's. Come on, Grandpa, he's only two! Oh, did I mention the tricycle, the hot wheels and two red wagons? Enough already!

Our neighbors have two rather large dogs that run along the fence. J and Wendell, J's dog, love to run along the fence with them—"puppies …

puppies," J screams as he runs after them. The dogs are bigger than J, now, but he still calls them "puppies."

Recently he discovered bugs, some good and some are not so good. "Jun bug …" he lets you know when he finds one. Bees are bad bugs and ants are for stepping on. The other day he and Grandpa caught a frog—how exciting. And he loves flags, insisting we must put out the flag when he comes over. "The flog … the flog." He shouts as he watches it wave in the wind. Now that he's three, he can say flag and he has a variety of them.

"Children make you want to start life over."
~Muhammad Ali

A Boy and His Dog

"Money will buy a pretty good dog but it won't buy the wag of his tail."
~Josh Billings

Wendell, part terror, part boxer, part mutt, was King of the castle, his master's pride and joy, until a little man came into his life. Now, there's a little person jumping on him, chasing him around the house and pulling his tail. Run Wendell run. Hide Wendell hide. No rest for Wendell the dog; he has to be in tip top shape to keep up or should we say, run from Little J. He has to protect his food, his toys—and his territory!

How do you explain to a two-year old that a dog is an animal and does not possess the same reasoning skills as humans? They do have emotions, but are simple creatures with instincts, and their emotions lack the complex thought process. They feel joy when they know you are pleased, they feel sad when someone dies or goes away. However, they do not premeditate; they do not plan ahead. They live for whatever is happening at the moment. Wait a minute; Little J doesn't have a complex thought pattern, either, and he lives for the moment, too. Maybe a relationship between dog and boy is a simple one.

Dogs pick up on the energy of their humans and believe me little J has plenty of energy; he's perpetual motion. Wendell can tell if the little man is hyper, nervous, scared, or calm. He prefers calm, although when you see the two of them playing together there is no "calm." Experts on training your dog will tell you that it is easier to communicate successfully with your dog if you use your body's energy rather than excited words. Little J has no problem there. However, if your dog does something wrong and you yell and scream at the dog or hit the dog it confuses the dog and J confuses Wendell a lot.

The day that Aunt Heidi's dog, Dudley, grabbed J's cookie and ate it was not a good example of communicating with your body's energy; screaming at the dog was all that J could do. It was his cookie darn it! When Dudley ate a second cookie that was it! J darted down the hall to complain to Aunt Heidi in not-so calm words, that "her" dog ate "his" cookie and that was unacceptable behavior. If you approach your dog in a very self-assured and calm manner to correct the dog at the moment he is doing the unwanted behavior with an assertive touch to their neck... this they understand. For the little man it's a forgiving hug around the neck. If you want your dog or your child to do or stop doing something, you need to first convince yourself it will happen. Stay calm and self-assured. Your dog will pick up on your emotion. Remember, the dog must be doing the deed at the moment of correction in order for you to successfully communicate that you are not happy with certain behavior. Wait a minute … are we talking about the little man or the big dog? Doesn't matter—calm and self-assurance works on both!

The best part of raising a dog and a boy together is nap time!

"No animal is so inexhaustible as an excited infant."
~Amy Leslie

Women

"Women gather together to wear silly hats, eat dainty food, and forget
how unresponsive their husbands are. Men gather to talk sports, eat
heavy food, and forget how demanding their wives are. Only where
children gather is there any real chance of fun."

~Mignon McLaughlin, *The Neurotic's Notebook*, 1960

Little J is a chick magnet. Women flock to him like flies to fly paper. He
learned to blow kisses early and definitely enjoys kissing the ladies.

We were out at a restaurant one time when J spotted a sweet young
lady sitting across from us; she couldn't have been more than two. "Blow
her kisses," I said. Wrong thing to say; next thing I knew the little man
was out of his booster seat darting across the room trying to give the little girl a kiss!

She didn't like it one bit and hid her head under mothers arms. Little
J wasn't about to give up.

"He's not shy is he?" The child's mother commented.

"Not today." I laughed.

Woman may think they have powers of flirtation but they have nothing over little J. He can flirt with the best of them. I like that he winks just
like his grandma—with both eyes shut!

So here is what you need to know little man about women:

"Female: One of the opposing, or unfair sex."

~Amerose Bierce

"Women, as some witty Frenchman once put it, inspire us with the
desire to do masterpieces, and always prevent us from carrying
them out."

~Oscar Wilder

"Women are always afraid of things that have to be divided."

~Honore De Balzac

"Every woman is a science."
    ~John Donne

"A woman never loafs—she shops, entertains and visits."
    ~E.W. Howe

"A woman is incapable of feeling love for an automobile."
    ~Bernard DeVoto

"The only way to understand a woman is to love her—and then it isn't necessary to understand her."
    ~Sydney Harris

Remember little man, grandma's are women. And we really love that last one—just love us!

Through the Eyes of a Child

"Kids: they dance before they learn there is anything that isn't music."
~William Stafford

You know what is really great about being a child? They look at life through inspiring eyes; everything they see and hear is astonishing to them.

They listen to the meadowlark sing.

They marvel at a star filled night and enjoy the beauty of a sunset.

They have time to chase a butterfly and to ask the question, "why?" When? "Who?" and "How come?"

The little man thinks dandelions are beautiful—he knows that weeds are for plucking and ice cream is for licking!

Children can sit down and read a book over and over again and never tire of the story. They laugh because they know it's OK to be silly once in awhile. They give you a hug even if you don't need one.

They count their blessings one by one and before they go to sleep at night they thank God for what He has done; they never worry about yesterday but look forward with great expectation to tomorrow.

Most important they say "Goodnight Moon. Goodnight Jesus."

Oh to look at life through the eyes of a child. Don't miss out on a blessing because you weren't looking or listening! Take time to look at life through a little one's eyes.

"The greatest blessing is created and enjoyed at the same moment."
~Epicurus

Fun Things for a Boy of Two to Do

Boy: a noise with dirt on it.
~*Not Your Average Dictionary*

I sure have learned a lot about being a grandma in the two years since Little J has come into my life. He has taught me all about all the fun things for a boy of two to do, like:

- Breaking crayons into a thousand little pieces.
- Throwing toys down the register then watching Daddy's frustration as he tries to get the toys out.
- Helping Dad take the screen door off so he can get the old refrigerator out and bring in the new one.
- Eating ice cream sandwiches for breakfast!
- Pulling the dog's tail and/or chasing the cat or doing both.
- Picking up sticks in the backyard.
- Putting Mommy's eye makeup on himself—then the dog!
- Jumping on Dad while he's still asleep. I bet Dad thinks that's fun, too.
- Helping Mom make pancakes for breakfast.
- Sticking plastic toys in the oven.
- Pushing the buttons on the dishwasher (pushes Mom's buttons).
- Opening and closing the microwave door until it goes "zap" and blows a fuse. (It cost Daddy $24 to fix it because he had to go out and buy the proper tools to get the back off.) This fun adventure is on the "naughty" list, too, and earns a time-out for Little J.
- Climbing up on the stool to play with water in the sink.
- Blowing bubbles.
- Throwing all his stuffed animals in a pile and then jumping on them!
- Jumping on the bed.
- Jumping on Grandma when she's not ready.
- Wrestling with anyone who will wrestle with him, but especially Grandma!

- Taking all the magnets off the refrigerator and hiding them around the house.
- Dumping the folded clothes out of the laundry basket so he can sit in the basket.
- Playing with powder and lotion—fun! (Also earns time-out).
- Eating string cheese and applesauce.
- Making his own pizza.
- Playing "monkey" with Grandma, bowling with Grandpa and playing basketball with Papa and/or going to basketball and football games.
- Helping Dad rack leaves. However, it's more fun to jump in the piles.
- Putting stickers on his shoes!
- Running through the lawn sprinkler. Going to the park.

Fiddle or faddle—just make sure you have fun doing it! And remember, Grandparents, "Fun is like life insurance; the older you get the more it costs!" ~Kin Hubbard

Learning to Talk

~Norman Douglas once said, "Everything is worth talking about."
Never truer for children.

"A child can ask questions that a wise man cannot answer."
~Author Unknown

I could hardly wait for Little J to talk. My friends who are grandmas told me not to rush the speech process because once they start talking its non-stop chatter.

J said "Mama, Dada, Papa and Nana" long before he could say Grandma or Grandpa. He first called Grandpa, "Pa." So naturally, I was breathlessly waiting to hear the word "Grandma." "Gram ... even Ma," would do. He was well into the terrible twos before I heard something that remotely resembled the word Grandma.

He used to call me Ya Ya. But then again, Ya Ya was the word he used to express just about anything he wanted to say. But then one day, it slipped out "Ger ..." so for weeks I was "Ger ... ."

4th of July we partied at my daughters. All day long, I was "Con ... nee. Con ... nee. Con ... nee." His mother went to kid's camp as a counselor in July of 2011. Daddy had to work so Ger and Nana were on babysitting patrol. I had him for three days—that was the week that it happened. "Gamma" came out of his mouth. I was so excited I did the Grandma dance! It was also the week that I noticed J was beginning to put words together.

"I hunger" he stood in the doorway and told me one day. It was off to McDonald's for a word reward. Oh, by the way he has mastered "McDonald's" and says it loud and clear. He knows what he wants when he gets there, "fries."

"Walk through life and talk to anybody." Persian Proverb. Once these little ones start talking the words seem to come fast and furious. And they manage to bring that Persian Proverb to life. J can say ele-phant and tele-phone now and Heidte for Aunt Heidi and calls her dog Dud-lay. He loves to identify the pictures when I read him *Goodnight Moon*. He gets pretty excited over the moon and the stars. But when I read "Hey diddle

diddle the cat and the fiddle … the cow jumped over the moon." He firmly shakes his head, "no..ooo." Everyone knows that cows can't jump over the moon, right?

When I ask him what would like for breakfast, he'll say "oatmeal." He lets me know when it's time for a snack. He's got that word down, pat, along with "pop and juice."

The other day he came to me and asked for an apple. He ran to the frig and came back to tell me "No apple. Applesauce?" he questioned.

There wasn't any of that, either, so Pa peeled him a carrot! It crunches the same, I guess. He can say, "Want candy" with no problem. Drink is still "dink" but he'll get it. He loves lee-men juice—(that's lemonade or lemon water) and believe it or not he likes rhubarb. He goes out to our rhubarb patch and asks for "barb." But my favorite words are "Luv you, Gamma … ." Now that definitely touches my heart.

"Children seldom misquote. In fact, they usually repeat word for word what you shouldn't have said."
~Author Unknown

Being a Grandma Just Happens

"Every time a baby is born, a grandma is made." That's one of my favorite quotes. I don't know who said it, but I really like it and I believe it's true.

We don't prepare for being grandma it just happens. A year with my adorable grandson flew by. Suddenly, he was a year old and walking and then in a blink of an eye, Little J turned two. In two years, I've learned so much about life as a grandma.

I've learned that completely washable is the way to go. That it's OK to have a trail of cookie crumbs that go from the kitchen to the sunroom.

I've learned that grandma's should always have a frig full of leftovers, fresh fruit, apple juice and lots of bananas! And a medicine cabinet with snoopy band aids—just in case.

I've been reminded that a kiss can cure almost anything and that I can do almost everything with two hands. (At least it's so in my grandson's eyes).

Grandmas are soft and tough at the same time. Spending time with Jeremiah has made me see that I haven't forgotten how to laugh or cry and I bet I can still color and play in the sandbox!

In a single tear a grandma can express joy, sorrow, pain and disappointment; Grandma "love" is freely given every day without conditions kind of like our heavenly Father's love for us. When you're in trouble you can always count on Grandma—and God.

Mothers, aunts, sisters and grandma's have their own specialness about them. They are unique; they come in all different sizes, shapes and colors. We can drive, fly, walk, run and email our grandchildren to show how much we care! I love talking to Little J over the IM and on the phone and via of Skype! I think He likes it, too.

Like a mother, a grandmother's heart keeps the world turning.

(This article first appeared in His Banner in May of 2010)

"Grandmothers are moms with frosting."
    ~Author Unknown

The Value of a Hug

"A hug is like a boomerang—you get it back right away."
~Bill Keane, *Family Circus*

My business partner and good friend died suddenly in February of 2010. I was devastated; there was so much going through my mind at the time … what to do with the business … how would I handle it without him? Did I even want to handle it without his input? My personal writing suffered … I couldn't concentrate and didn't know how to handle my emotions. I went through some days in a complete daze—the only thing that saved me was a hug from the little man. I just couldn't be sad when he was around. His hugs cheered me up. His antic's chased away my blues just what a hug is supposed to do. "… A hug can soothe a small child's pain (and an adult's, too) and bring a rainbow after the rain." ~Author not known.

The hug; there's no doubt in my mind we scarcely could survive without it.

"Hugs are great for fathers and mothers, sweet for sisters, swell for brothers; and chances are your favorite aunt love them, too; heads of states are not above them. A hug can say, 'It's OK to cry, I'm here for you. Don't worry everything's going to be alright; no matter what we'll get through this together.' A hug can break the language barrier and make your travel so much merrier. No need to fret about your store of them; the more you give, the more there is of them. So stretch those arms without delay and give someone a hug today."
~Author Unknown

It's been proven by scientists and doctors alike that hugs are therapeutic. There are many types of hugs. I've probably given and received them all … hello and goodbye hugs. Enthusiastic hugs that you might give to someone you haven't seen in a while. Romantic hugs, comforting hugs, cheering hugs, hugs of accomplishment. Then there's the sideways hug which is essentially a one-armed embrace that shows friendliness and acceptance—I call this the Hawkins hug. No matter what type of hug you give or receive, a hug is a hug and it carries emotional benefits. But the best hug of all is the no reason—I love you Grandma hug!

"A hug delights and warms and charms that must be why God gave us arms."
~Author Unknown

Dancing to the Beat of His Own Drum (Or Singing)

"Singing is a way of releasing an emotion that you sometimes can't portray when you're acting. And music moves your soul, so music is the source of the most intense emotions you can feel. When you hear a song and you're reacting it's incredible. But when you're singing a song and you're re-acting it's even more incredible."
~Amanda Seyfried

When I was a kid growing up on the farm, my mother would often make Friday night talent night—it most always involved music and dancing. I would play my accordion. My brothers would get out their trumpets—we'd make up songs and sing and dance. I remember sitting in the stairway singing Connie Francis songs because I liked the way my voice echoed in the stairway and partly because I didn't want anyone to see me singing! And, I loved to dance around my bedroom; it always made me feel better about myself. I bought a piano when my children were small and used to make up songs for them on Saturday afternoons. You could say I started my career as a writer writing country songs and songs for kids on the piano.

Little J loves music as well. He loves to sing and dance; to watch that incredible emotion come alive in him is something special to behold. He comes by this love of music naturally; his mother sings in the church choir and on occasion with the praise team. J's father plays a little guitar (very little he says) and has been known to make up a song or two of his own on the piano.

J can turn just about anything into a drum; the trash can in the bathroom. Pots and pans, the register, the footstool, the bird feeder in the backyard. Sometimes he actually gets a beat going. (Sorry we broke the morocco, Mom). He has a Fisher Price piano, two guitars (one at our house) and a play microphone that he doesn't really care about—he'd rather have the real thing.

J sings at the table, in the bathroom, in his car seat on the way to Grandma's and I have no doubt that he'll eventually be singing in church on the stage with his mother.

I've also seen him dance on the table, followed by time out.

"Dancing faces you towards Heaven, whichever direction you turn."
~Terri Guillemets

Stopping to Pick the Flowers

"A rose can say "I love you", orchids can enthrall, but a weed bouquet
in a chubby fist, yes that says it all."
~Author Unknown

There is nothing so thrilling to a mother and/or a grandma then to get a
bouquet of hastily picked half-dead dandelions, except of course, if there's
a bumble bee attached! The little man hasn't quite learned the difference
between a flower and a weed, but I am confident that in time he will. In
the meantime, in spite of the fact that I am allergic to this golden yellow
pesky weed, I am perfectly happy to put my dandelions in a tiny juice glass
and proudly display it, one sneeze at a time, on the counter in the kitchen.

How can I not be proud when one little man runs so hardily across
the lawn as fast as he can into Pa's field of weeds to pick for me the perfect
flower? He hasn't even learned how to say, "I picked a flower for you," yet,
but I am confident in time he will be able to say that and more. No matter how many beautiful flowers he'll come to know, some day, none will
be as dear to me then when he first plucked a weed gone astray; when the
little man knelt down and picked for me a dandelion one hot summer day.
Now, frogs are another story.

One July day while Grandpa was weeding the garden, he and Little J
came upon a frog. J chased that frog up and down the garden until he (the
frog) disappeared under the deck. That was fine with me. This grandma
was nowhere near ready to compliment the little man on such a find. He
went on to look for June bugs and was quick to come and get me when he
would find one. (I loathe June bugs.) I casually mentioned to Pa one day
that we had a problem with ants. Little J must have overheard that remark
and has been stepping on ants ever since. "All gone," he says. He's learning
the difference between good bugs and bad bugs. Bees and mosquitoes are
bad bugs. We don't pick bees. We don't pick ants—but we do pick beautiful yellow weeds for Grandma!

"The miracles of nature do not seem miracles because they are so common. If no one had ever seen a flower, even a dandelion would be the most startling event in the world."

~Author unknown

Cleaning the House

"Cleaning your house while your kids are still growing up is like shoveling the walk before it stops snowing."
~Phyllis Diller

The Oxford Dictionary of Proverbs, edited by Jennifer Speake, Oxford University Press has this to say abut cleanliness:

Next in this proverb means "immediately following," as in serial order. Cf. [1605 Bacon *Advancement of Learning* ii. 44] Cleanness' of bodie was euer esteemed to proceed from a due reuerence to God.

Slovenliness is no part of religion. "Cleanliness is indeed next to godliness." [*a* 1791 Wesley *Works* (1872) VII. 16]

"Cleanliness is next to Godliness." The latter quality, as displayed in a Russian devotee, is more allied with dirt than anything else. [1876 F. G. Burnaby *Ride to Khiva* x.]

The hospital staff had a thing about personal cleanliness, next to godliness, you might say. [1979 C. Egleton *Backfire* i.]

But a $6,000 shower curtain? Even if cleanliness is next to godliness, isn't that kind of steep? [2002 *Washington Post* 14 Aug. C2]

Next to every good man is a woman and a child with a broom in one hand and a dustpan in the other! Little J loves to help his Mama clean. Can you imagine how long it must take her to sweep the floor when the little man is holding on to the broom or is trying to carry the collected dust to the waste basket!

I solved that problem. I gave him a rag and told him that his job is to dust the furniture. After which we make the beds but not before we jump on them and wrestle in them!

After a few minutes of rough-housing, I would tell J, "All done." And I would remake the bed. "No more jumping on the bed, you little monkey," said I.

Several minutes would pass ... I would hear J jumping on the bed again.

"J were you jumping on the bed again?"

"Ya ya," he would say.

"No more monkeys jumping on the bed." I'd tell him. "You might fall off and bump your head."

The next time I not only found the little man in the bed but several of his stuffed animals, including two monkeys!

"Monkey's on the bed." He sings, "Bumps on the head."

I didn't see those monkeys on the bed. I only saw the little man.

"The art of being wise is knowing what to overlook."
~William James

Responding to a Tug

"If you haven't time to respond to a tug at your pants leg, your schedule is too crowded."

~Robert Brault

Almost as soon as he was only enough to stand, crawl and then walk, Little J would grab your hand or tug on your arm or leg when he wanted you to do something. Usually, he wanted you to come with him down the hall into his room to play with his toys or read books to him. Grandparents, have you noticed what joy they take showing you their toys or in knowing you are watching them play? I always have time to watch and to play.

The older J got the more innovative his games were. Sometimes, we would build with his Lego blocks or read books about birds or we would sing songs and bang on his drum but is favorite game is car crash. We line up all the cars on the footstool in his room, drive them to the edge, watch them crash, and then call the "helicopter police." To call the police is my job. Sometimes J would play this game by himself. I would sit in the rocker and thumb through a magazine, but when the crash occurred, I had to stop reading and yell, "helicopter police." The police would come immediately (sometimes this entailed a quick run down the hall and back) right all the upside down cars and we'd start the game all over again. We couldn't play "going to the gas station or to the grocery store" it was always "car crash and helicopter police." I honestly don't know where this game came from as I much preferred to play rock star or song writer on his piano or put stickers in the sticker book or make up a poem or color a picture or tickle the little man.

Now that he's three and driving (his pink and purple car) he likes to crash into my car or my Amigo. "Car crash," I have to say. "Grandma don't like to crash."

"Call the police and the insurance man," he says. (His mother and his Grandpa had car crashes, thus the police and insurance man were called; that's my theory.) An important lesson to learn: "If you can't take the heat, don't tickle the dragon." I have no idea what it means; I read it on the Internet and thought it fit here. What I've really learned here is that no matter what the time of day is when I feel that tug on my hand, I take time to look and listen and learn to follow where the little man leads, because I am still learning and what a great adventure learning with Little J has turned out to be! I'm glad I have enough wisdom to respond to a tug.

"Of all parts of wisdom the practice is the best."
~John Tillotson

Bed Time Games

"Any kid will run any errand for you if you ask at bedtime."
~Red Skelton

Don't you just love the bed time games that little people play? I'm too hot. I'm too cold. I need a drink. I have to go to the potty. I'm not tired. They never are.

My favorite bedtime story is one my friend Julie told me about her grandson, Little E. She'd do all the right things ... warm milk, a nice bath, a good story, a lovely song, prayers ... then she'd tuck him in. E would close his eyes, but as soon as Grandma was out of the room, he would start. "Grandma, my toe isn't covered ... Grandma my elbow is sticking out ... Grandma my blanket fell on the floor ..." Ah, kids and bed time. As he grew older, Little J used the same excuses.

It's important that parents establish a bedtime routine early on. And it's just as important that grandparents follow the rules. We have a routine when J spends the night with Grandma. A bath, a snack, two books, one of which is "Goodnight Moon"—it's really a great book and beneficial to introducing sleep. My routine also includes a lullaby CD and of course, his God bless prayers. "Good bless Mommy and Da Da and Wendell and Jinx and Nana and Papa and Uncle Matthew and Gamma and Pa and Aunt Heidte and Uncle Dave and Dudlay and Aunt Jill and Uncle Nate and Tylo and Ly-d-ia and Mimi ..." it goes on and on until Grandma cuts in with a God Bless everyone. Once we put the lullaby music on, there's no talking—it works Grandma goes right to sleep! The little man—now that's another story.

"It's amazing how few people are conscious of the importance of the art of lying in bed." ~Lin Yutang. This art my grandson has net yet mastered. I'm not sure he ever will, at least not at Grandma's house. There's way too much to do to think about a good sleep. As for me give me a bed and a good book and I'm happy. "Goodnight Moon. Goodnight noises everywhere. Goodnight little man."

"Goodnight, Grandma ... sleep if you can."

"The waking have one common world, but the sleeping turn aside
each into a world of his own."

~Heraclitus

Traveling With Children

"In America there are two classes of travel-first class, and with children."
~R. Benchley

Before you leave on that great American vacation, take a look at these ten commandments of vacationing. They aren't written in stone, but they might prove helpful when making travel plans.

1. Thou shalt not leave home without considerable prayer. (I always pray I won't have to go.)

2. Thou shalt not take the children on every vacation. One every three to six years is plenty of family togetherness. Children do not go on vacation to have fun; they go to drive their parent's nuts.

3. Thou shalt not leave the driveway without double checking the oven, the lights, the locks, the garden hose. One year we left the outside water spigot running. Our son proudly kept this information to himself for over 100 miles!

4. Thou shalt not position the seat kicker behind the driver; it will irritate him immensely and make him very angry.

5. Thou shalt not leave home without plenty of aspirin, which helps thee cope with hysteria when thy daughter casually leans over the seat and tells you that she thinks she either left the curling iron on or the shower running—or both!

6. Thou shalt not tell the driver as he's crossing the Michigan/Indiana border that you forgot to mention the strange noise you heard coming from the car's engine last week.

7. Thou shalt not mention to anyone over 30 that the extra case in the trunk contains the family cat. (I was wondering what that scratching noise was for the last 88 miles) I hope they didn't put the hamster in the trunk with the cat!

8. Thou shalt not express to these same people that your little brother spilled red pop on the velvet upholstery. Keep it to thyself until the stain dries.

9. Thou shalt not come down with measles, whooping cough, or a fever one day into the vacation. This is against the rules.

10. Thou shalt do all things without grumbling and disputing

—because God says so. (Philippians 2:14)
From Connie's book Sailing Through Life In A Rowboat.

"And that's the wonderful thing about family travel: it provides you with experiences that will remain locked forever in the scar tissue of your mind."
~Dave Barry

Building Character

"It is easier to build strong children than to repair broken men."
~Frederick Douglass

My mother once told me that enduring life's trials produces character and makes you strong. If that's true, then I have plenty of character as I've had my share of trials over the years.

Building character isn't a class in school, but it should be. Every adult in a child's life should have a hand in building that child's character. But how do you teach a toddler the traits he or she will need to build strong character?

It's been over 30 years since I've had to worry about such things but here I am Grandma looking into the most beautiful, teasing blue eyes.

How do parents expect a Grandma to say no? Or to work on character building with them? Respect, courtesy and empathy were not fun topics of discussion for Grandma. But sometimes, ready or not, even grandparents are thrusts into the role of building character. I truly believe that we build character in our children and grandchildren by example, by being honest in our daily living, loving, and respectful towards the opinions of others. Most important character is about opening your mind and your heart.

Jeremiah is quite a character and apparently is all ears when he hears us talk about him.

Jeremiah: "I a character, Gamma."

Grandma: "And what is a character?" I ask.

Jeremiah: "I funny." He wrinkles up his sweet little nose.

"Few men realize that their life, the very essence of their character, their capabilities and their audacities, are only the expression of their belief in the safety of their surroundings."
~Joseph Conrad

Respecting Others

"Surely it's not about who or what you know in this world; it's about
being a good person and having respect for others."
~Unknown author

Respect, what does this word really mean? And how do we teach our children the value of respect? It is to show regard for the worth of someone else as well as yourself. If you don't respect yourself you can't respect others. It is to be tolerant of others and their ideas and opinions. So respect starts with yourself and in taking pride in your achievements and your potential. It also fosters self-control of your actions and emotions so as not to hurt other people's feelings. I think respect is best taught by example.

One day, I was happily looking through some of J's books while he played on the floor beside me, when J suddenly came up to me and swooshed the books to the floor. "That is not nice," I scolded. "Why are you throwing these books on the floor? I waited for an answer. "Grandma was reading those books ... you hurt Grandma's feelings when you won't share your books with me and throw them on the floor. It's not a nice thing to do. It's disrespectful." Not that J understood what the word "disrespectful" meant at that time in his life, but I used the word anyway.

I didn't care that J was only two. As an author it is very important to me that my grandchildren develop a healthy respect for books. Books can take you on so many adventures and introduce you to so many new possibilities. I used to tell my children, "If you tear the pages or destroy your books, an adventure will be lost to you." They believed me. I was hoping on this particular day that Little J would believe me, too. He gave me his sad face and began to pick up the books. A sad face when you're only two is equal to an apology at least it was as far as this grandma was concerned.

"Be beautiful if you can, wise if you want to... but be respected that
is essential."
~Anna Gould

Honesty

"If you tell the truth you don't have to remember anything."
~Mark Twain

We must teach our children to be honest, to speak what is good and what is true by explaining to them that it's not okay to do something sneaky just because they can get away with it. Character building begins by consistently holding up our little ones to a high standard of ethical behavior. The building of ones character continues with honesty.

"J, who broke Grandma's angel? Did you break it?"
"I not sure."
How can you not hug a cherub?

"Make yourself an honest man, and then you may be sure there is one less rascal in the world."
~Thomas Carlyle

Courtesy

"Teach children to be polite and courteous in the home, and, when he grows up, he will never be able to edge his car onto a freeway."
~Author unknown

As parents and grandparents we need to sit an example for our kids by being courteous and respectful to everyone we meet. Children don't always "do as you say" but you better believe they will "do as you do." Those little eyes are watching you.

Whenever a child acts rude to anyone, ask them how they would feel if someone were rude to them. J's parents constantly work on this character trait by teaching J that he needs to be nice to the dog, that it's rude to chase Wendell, pull his tail and jump on him. It's a never ending job because for some reason J likes to torment the dog or maybe he just enjoys time out. However, the older he gets the better he is at being "courteous."

I use a cane. J knows that Grandma has a bad leg and walks different, that he needs to pick up his toys so Grandma doesn't trip and fall. If I do stumble a bit, he says, "You OK, Gamma?"

It's important that we teach our children to take an interest in kids who are different from them, whether it's another culture, a disability or the way they look—it's what courtesy is all about.

"Greatness is so often a courteous synonym for great success."
~Philip Guedalla quotes (English Historian, 1889-1944)

A Sunday School Lesson on Love

"Love makes everything lovely; hate concentrates itself on one thing, hatred."

~George McDonald

Susie came home from Sunday school all excited.

"We had a new girl in class today," she told her mother.

"What's her name?"

"Yoko. She's from Japan."

"That's nice," her mother said.

"Some of the kids made fun of her."

"Why would they do that?" Her mother asked.

"Because she looks funny. Her eyes are slanted and her skin is darker than ours."

"What did the teacher do?"

"She baked cookies."

"Cookies?" Susie's mother questioned.

"Gingerbread men," Susie explained. "Some had white frosting on them. Some had chocolate. We all got to taste them."

"Then what happened?"

"They all tasted the same," Susie said. "They were all very, very good. Teacher says that's how God sees us—all the same. All very, very good. She said 'Jesus loves all the children of the world. Red and yellow, black and white, that we are all precious in His sight.' It was our Sunday school lesson."

"What do you think it means?"

"That we should love everyone no matter what color their frosting is!"

As adults we can learn something from this simple, but profound, lesson—to love no matter what—not just on Christmas or Valentine's Day, but every day. In case we forget, God reminds us in I John 4:7, "Beloved, love one another for love is of God."

(From the book Sailing Through Life In A Rowboat)

Decision Making

"Do not plant your dreams in the field of indecision, where nothing
ever grows but the weeds of what-if."
  ~Dodinsky

Learning to make decisions can start as early as the toddler stage of life, if
not before. I like that Jeremiah's parents give him choices whenever they
can. Not only is it important to give children a choice, but it's equally important to hold them to their decisions.

Little J wanted a snack. His mother told him he had a choice. He could
have a sucker or a cookie. He chooses a sucker, a yellow one. He ate half
of it, held it up to his mother and said, "Yucky, want cookie."
  Don't tell me this two-year old mind isn't thinking.

"I can make 'good' choices when I want to; sometimes, I choose not to!"
  ~Anonymous

Empathy

"Be nice to people." That is the lesson my grandmother taught me.
A little empathy goes a long way ..."
~Simran Khurana

Encourage your kids to keep their hearts open. It can be especially difficult when someone hurts their feelings. Emphasize that they should feel
sorry for hurtful people because those people are expressing their own
pain by being mean to others. Point out all the caring people in their lives
and encourage your kids and grandkids to think of them whenever someone hurts their feelings.

J loves to come and spend the day with Grandma. As soon as he comes
through the door he tells his parents, "You go home. I stay."

"J," I say. "That's not nice to say. Telling Mommy and Daddy to go home
hurts their feelings."

"I sorry." That cherub face again.

"Can we wrestle now, Gamma?"

"Only your compassion and your loving kindness are invincible, and
without limit."
~Thich Nhat Hanh

Helping Others

"I am only one, but I am one. I cannot do everything, but I can do something. And I will not let what I cannot do interfere with what I can do."
  ~Edward Everett Hale

One thing my mother taught me when I was growing up was the importance of helping others. She did this by exposing my brothers and me to people less fortunate, although at the time, we thought we were the less fortunate. I'm sure we complained when it came to doing charitable works but as an adult, I am grateful for the new experiences I gained from helping others. It made me a better person. As a Christian I am convinced that every time we show our children the value of helping others the world becomes a better place.

Little J is a bit young to grasp this concept but he loves to help. If I'm doing laundry he pulls his little stool up to the washer and helps me put the clothes in one sock at a time. What used to take 20 minutes now seems to take an hour! J likes to help Grandpa make a cake and he loves to help his Aunt Heidi with Mac & Cheese. If Mommy is doing something in the kitchen, the bathroom or J's room, you can bet he's right there helping, except when it comes to picking up his toys then he's no where to be found!

I leave you with this thought. In order to train up a child in the way he should go, try traveling down his road, sometime. And most important forget the character flaws, because, "The art of being wise is in knowing what to over look." ~William James

"No one ever changes his character from the time he is two years old; nay, I might say, from the time he is two hours old."
  ~William Hazlitt

Trouble—We've got Trouble

"The way out of trouble is never as simple as the way in."
~E.W. Howe

There can't be another crisis this week, my schedule is completely full. And yet, trouble will somehow find its way into your schedule. My daughter-in-law was packing to go to Kids Camp or at least she was trying to. Two year-old J had an agenda of his own, like stuffing tweezers down the bathroom sink. Dragging his mattress off the bed and dumping toys all over his room gets to be boring. He tore into the kitchen when he heard his mother open the dishwasher, that's when he broke one of Mom's new glasses. At this point, she sent him to his room for some time out. What's a boy to do? How about stuffing toys down the heat register. All of these activities in less than an hour; is it any wonder moms get frustrated.

Keeping a toddler out of trouble is no easy task. I never did quite figure out how the little man was able to climb up into his closet and drag a box down from the shelve, a box by the way that contained glass candle holders, smack them together and break them. That was the day he came running down the hall, "Boo boo need band aide," Johnson & Johnson will never run out of customers as long as there are toddlers running amuck. You might want to hide your jewelry and your make-up, keep the bathroom door closed and a secure lid on the garbage can.

J has had more bruises, scrapes and bumps than a grandma can count. His first Christmas he had a black eye because he ran into the corner of Dad's computer. As soon as he learned that sidewalks were for running, he fell and scraped his knee. There have been cut fingers, silvers and swollen lips—and he's barely two! Trouble just seems to find this little man. Trouble we got trouble right here in our city … it rhymes with play and his name is J.

There are some households in which careful disorder is the norm and that household usually holds a toddler within its walls.

"One of the advantages of being disorderly is that one is constantly making exciting discoveries."

~A. A. Milne

"Our greatest glory consists not in never falling, but in rising every time we fall."

~Oliver Goldsmith

Going to the Mall

"Shopping is a woman thing. It's a contact sport like football. Women enjoy the scrimmage, the noisy crowds, the danger of being trampled to death, and the ecstasy of the purchase."
~Erma Bombeck

Going to the Mall is shopping utopia for most women. Have you ever noticed that women will flock to a sale and will buy anything that is "one to a customer"? And why is it that no matter what line you're in the other lines seemed to be moving faster.

The other day I went into K-Mart to buy some T-shirts for my husband and came out with an outfit for myself, and two kitchen gadgets that I have yet to figure out what they are.

J's second birthday party was held at the Mall. The Mall has both a McDonald's and a play room. As much as the little man loves his nuggets and fries he loves playing more and gobbled down his food so he could run to the play area.

He took off before his father could catch him. When he finally caught up to him there was a mild scolding.

"Jeremiah, you don't go off without taking someone with you."

J ran over, grabbed his cousin's hand (also two years old) and headed back to the playroom! Now is that a smart boy?

Little J didn't stay put long. While his cousin continued to explore the ins and outs of the climbing cubes in the play area, J was out the door darting down the isles of the Mall, his Papa close on his heels.

For Little J the Mall is an amusement park of sorts. So much to do and see; so many doors to dash in and out of. I hope he grows up to be an excellent shopper.

"The only reason a great many American families don't own an elephant is that they have never been offered an elephant for a dollar down and easy weekly payments."
~Mad Magazine

A Day at the Beach

"Don't grow up too quickly, lest you forget how much you love the beach."

~Author Michelle Held

Beach balls, umbrellas, water toys, water vest, swimmies … I think we are just about ready for a day at the beach.

J is as fast in the water as he is on land and shows no fear. I can barely keep up with him on land, let alone in the water. The best I can do is to sit in my lawn chair at the water's edge and "Yell, come back Little J."

If you are planning a beach vacation in the near future and you have a toddler tagging along with you the key word is to be "prepared." Here are a few tips on taking your toddler to the beach

Going to the beach is an exciting time. Especially if you are like me and live no where near a beach. Since J came into my life, I learned that there is a big difference in taking a toddler to the beach over taking your older children or even an infant. It's been 35 years since I've been to the beach with kids. I've forgotten what it takes.

The main thing to remember when taking a toddler to the beach is naptime. Grandma will need to rest so be sure to bring a reclining lawn chair. Seriously, if your toddler still takes naps then it is highly likely that you will need to continue their regular nap routine. This excitement of being at the beach can quickly tire a toddler out and Grandma, too. So if it's even remotely possible for your toddler to take a nap then I suggest you put them down for one. This will make for a happier toddler and an even happier family. I know Grandma's happy to nap. Did I mention a reclining lawn chair?

Sun block is a necessary part of going to the beach vacation, especially for a toddler and Grandma. Their skin is still very thin and highly suscep- tible to nasty sunburn. Mine—a bit wrinkled; I don't need over exposure to the sun to make those worry lines more prominent. Always be aware of the time of day and when the last time you applied sun bock was. If your toddler is having a great time playing in the water make sure that you dry them off before applying more sun block and allow that sun block to dry completely before allowing your toddler back into the water. And don't forget some extra sun block for Grandma! We have crumpled, delicate skin!

Beware of sand. Sand is a necessary annoyance when you go to the beach but it can be harmful to a toddler if not watched closely. The main thing to watch for is sand in the eyes and in the snack bag! Did I mention the importance of bringing along some tasty snacks … orange and apple slices for the little one and a glass of something very cold for Grandma! Keep in mind, it's inevitable that all children will at least taste sand on their first trip to the beach but watch closely to make sure that the sand does not get rubbed into their eyes. Especially if you have a tired toddler who is only trying to rub their little tired eyes with a sand covered hand. Have you gotten a hug with sand-covered hands—it's a bit gritty but none the less a hug. Oh, don't forego building a sand castle, that's the best part of the beach. Now where did I put my sand shovel?

Beach toys are a necessity, especially, if you want your toddler to be entertained and to enjoy the beach. A rather large inner tube for Grandma will suffice; one with a drink holder would be nice. One thing I've learned being grandma is to bring a big purse! I can stuff favorite toys, an extra towel and a blanket into one very large purse. My purse is a toy onto itself. It has kept the little man entertained at church, at the Mall and at the beach! Unless you plan to run all over the beach chasing down a two-year old, then make sure you bring that BIG purse. And make sure you don't bring along any toys that you would not want sand to get on because sand gets on EVERYTHING.

Umbrellas are needed on a hot, sunny day at the beach. If you have the money to invest in your own umbrella and you plan to go to the beach often then I suggest going ahead and buying your own beach umbrella. We purchased ours for only $20. Grandma doesn't go to the beach without it! Of course, J has to open and close it—that's the best part of an umbrella in his mind. Oh, and beware of the outside showers because they are cold. Sure, it's a hot summer day and you are covered in sand. What's better than just rinsing the sand off of you and your toddler before heading back to the car? Even though it's a hot summer day the water coming out of those outside showers can be ice cold. Most toddlers do not appreciate cold water being showered over them even if it's for washing that sticky sand off. So just a little warning about the cold showers.

J is at the age where his curiosity often gets the better of him. So, keep an eye out for sea creatures. Any moving critter draws J's attention but there are many that will hurt your little one. Jellyfish can wash up on shore and their sting is so dangerous. Crabs can be around if it's later in the day and you would not want one of those attached to your toddler, or yourself for that matter.

Always remember to bring things like extra clothes, snacks, bottled water, soft drinks, cooler, camera and anything else that will make your trip to the beach easier and keep you from having to run back and forth to your motel room, camper and or vehicle. If you bring sippy cups it's easier if you are the one to hold it to give your toddler a drink. They will have sand on their hands and that sand will get all over their cups and it will just spread. Sand can and will get all over everything that you take to the beach so watch your food and drinks closely. (Yes, I'm a little obsessed with sand—I don't particularly enjoy it.) I do suggest bringing bottled water, not just to drink, but to wash other things off with. Make sure to bring a nice big blanket for Grandma and J to lie on. And don't forget the umbrella to keep the blanket cooler. Ah, now we can count our Z's in comfort.

In the end, enjoy your beach experience with your toddler. They are only little once so make sure that you enjoy it as much as they do. The wonder of the world is a joy to watch through the eyes of your toddler. But for me the best part of going to the beach is coming home!

"The waters wear the stones."
~The Book of Job 14:19

Bad Hair Days

"Babies haven't any hair. Old men's heads are just as bare; from the cradle to the grave lies a haircut and a shave."
~Samuel Goodman Hoffenstein

" ... Gimme a head with hair, long beautiful hair, shining, gleaming, streaming, flaxen, waxen. I love hair. Give me down to there hair; shoulder length or longer ... here baby, there Mama Everywhere Daddy Daddy ... Hair, hair, hair, hair, hair, hair, hair. Flow it, show it long as God can grow it my hair ..."
~From the musical "Hair"

While some babies come into the world bald, Jeremiah was born with dark, spiky hair that provided him with plenty of personality. ~Shana Alexander said of hair, "Hair brings one's self-image into focus; it is vanity's proving ground. Hair is terribly personal, a tangle of mysterious prejudices."

Life is an endless struggle full of frustrations and challenges, one of which is hair, but eventually you find a hair stylist you like! "Beauty draws us with a single hair" wrote Alexander Pope. Most toddlers have little choice in the matter of hair and/or hair stylists, their mothers do the styling. So J has gone from "spiky Mikey" to an impish pixie, a bad butch and a crop close to the head cut—just like Daddy. Throughout these changes he has ever remained our Little J.

~Fran Lebowitz said once, "Violet will be a good color for hair at just about the same time that brunette becomes a good color for flowers." Well, Fran, that time is here. It used to be when you were first learning to color, hair wasn't purple or green—that's not true anymore. Just the other day I saw kids with bright pink, spiked hair walking down the street as if pink hair was the most natural order of hair color. Dolly Parton said she was never offended by all the dumb-blonde jokes because she knew that she wasn't dumb, "And I also know I'm not blonde."

Make no mistake, two or twenty, " ... hair is vitally personal to children. They weep vigorously when it is cut for the first time; no matter how it grows, bushy, straight or curly; they feel they are being shorn of a part of their personality." ~Charles Chaplin. So you gotta love these first-time haircut pictures of small children sitting on boards in the barber shop or on their mother's laps at the beauty salon, or standing in Nana's kitchen because it takes four to do the job—three holding, one cutting. And when it's tearfully over—it's over. Now where's the promised red sucker!

"Experience is a comb which nature gives us when we are bald."
~Proverb

Angry Eyebrows

"Anger raises invention, but also over heats the oven."
~Lord Halifax

Long before "angry birds" there was angry eyebrows. Two things infants learn immediately: To cry is to be feed. Not to be feed is to get angry. Little J, like most infants, wanted to eat when he was hungry and if you didn't feed him on schedule his piercing wails let you know that he wasn't happy. If wailing wasn't enough, he'd bunch up his eyebrows, which soon became known to anyone around him as his angry eyebrows.

When J doesn't get his way, we get angry eyebrows. According to many mental health care experts, anger has three components. Emotional, expression and action. The first component is the emotion itself, defined as an affective or arousal state, or a feeling experienced when a goal is blocked or needs are frustrated, very prevalent in the "terrible two's." Children are learning so much during this stage in their lives that frustration comes quickly and isn't always easily overcome.

The second component of anger is its expression. Some children vent or express anger through facial expressions, crying, sulking, or talking, but do little to try to solve a problem or confront the provocateur. At this stage of the game they have no idea what to do or how to solve a problem—it's easier to cry about it. I'm 60 something and I still cry about it.

It was Easter morning … Aunt Heidi made cheesy biscuits for breakfast but before the little man could eat his, Dudley, jumped up and grabbed it. Not knowing what else to do, J sat on the floor and cried. Crying quickly turn to frustration which turned into a full-blown temper tantrum.

"Stop screaming," Aunt Heidi shouted. "I can't understand you when you are screaming." The little man continued to scream, pointing to the dog. It was plain to see Auntie was getting equally frustrated.

J was simply looking for a solution to his problem, and seeking comfort from his pain. Grandma to the rescue—I didn't need a biscuit, anyway. End of story.

The third component of the anger experience is understanding and evaluating the emotion. Because the ability to regulate the expression of anger is linked to an understanding of the emotion (Zeman & Shipman, 1996), and because children's ability to reflect on their anger is somewhat limited, children need guidance in understanding and managing their feelings of anger. *(Helping Children Cope with Anger by Marian Marion, PhD)* Whenever J has a melt-down, all we as adults need to do is figure out what he is angry or upset about and fix it. Isn't that we are supposed to do?

"If you want to see what your children can do, stop giving them things."
~Norman Douglas

Teach them to fend for themselves, to think for themselves, to create, to imagine and to understand that with anger comes consequences. Children learn more by example than they do by criticism. They watch, they see—they do. They listen—they speak. So be careful what you say and do because your children are watching you.

"Do not let the sun go down on your anger."
~Ephesians 4:25

Books and Reading

"A classic is something that everybody wants to have read and nobody wants to read."
~Mark Twain

Some people keep the classics on their coffee table simply to appear well
read. I'm an author. I've been reading books since I was in kindergarten and
writing them almost as long. My mother said I was born with ink in my
blood and a pen in my hand. To me books are a world within themselves,
a place where you dare to escape the ordinary doldrums of life. Between
the covers of a good book lies adventure, intrigue, humor, romance and
mystery. I love books that tickle my fancy and entice me to go beyond the
first 10 pages. I cannot imagine a more pleasant way to spend a rainy day
then curled up with a good book—unless I'm curled up with a good book
like *Cat in The Hat*, with Little J.

One of my goals as J's grandma is to teach him a love and a respect
for books and to appreciate the places that he can go, between the covers
of a book, whether to Old Mother Hubbard's cupboard or traveling with
Gulliver. Whenever my children were bored I'd tell them to read a book.
Weekly trips to the library were awesome experiences; we'd come home
with bags of books. I took a Children's Lit class in college; our assign-
ment was to read 30 children's books a week. My kids thought they were
in heaven that every night I'd read one or two new books to them, wonderful books like *Where The Wild Things Are* by Maurice Sendax or the
Little Bear books by Else Holmelund Minarik. Occasionally, I would write
stories just for them but I could never quite compete with *Hop on Socks*.

The more children read, the better they become at reading. The more I
read to J, the more he'll want me to read. It's as simple as that. Right now
his favorite books at Grandma's house are: *The Chicken Book* and *Goodnight
Moon*. The more young children are read to, the greater their interest in
mastering reading. Reading out loud exposes children to proper gram-
mar and phrasing. It enhances the development of their spoken language
skills, their ability to express themselves verbally. Reading to them in the

womb is not out of the question. Even the fetus responds to the sound of a human voice.

I love the feeling I get when Little J climbs up on my lap with a book in hand—it's a wonderful love feeling. And I know that each time we reach for a new book to read, I am helping to enrich J's life, opening up for him new worlds to explore.

So cat in the hat move over—Grandma Connie's here! And she's ready to read and write a good book!

"Anyone who says they have only one life to live must not know how to read a book."
~Author Unknown

First Time for Everything

"A great man is the man who does a thing for the first time."
~Alexander Smith

I saw something the other day that I have never seen before. I was just finishing breakfast at a local restaurant when a group of about 20 people came in and they had a dog. Not a seeing-eye dog. A little fluffy dog on a leash, and the server seated the group with the dog. This was a first for me, other than a seeing-eye dog, I have never seen a dog in a sit down restaurant before and for the life of me I couldn't figure out why it was allowed. So I did a little looking on the Internet found a couple of neat sites that provide assistance dogs for the disabled and dogs for people with special needs. "Well, I'll be," I thought to myself, "There's a first time for everything."

First time events must be stressful for infants, don't you agree? The first time they roll over without help, crawl, utter that first word, take that first step. Realize that they are no longer a prisoner in their own crib that they can climb out!

This is one of my favorite quotes by James Barrie, "When the first baby laughed for the first time, the laugh broke into a thousand pieces and they all went skipping about, and that was the beginning of fairies." There's a quote from Peter Pan that says when you stop believing in fairies they begin to drop dead one fairy at a time and with them go our fairy tales, our sense to make believe when reality just won't do. The Tooth Fairy, Easter Bunny and Santa Claus are all figments of our wonderful imagination— we really can't have much fun in the world without them. And why would we want to?

There is an old Chinese Proverb that says, "All things **at first** appear difficult but we should never give up doing what must come first." First tooth, first grin, first step, first day at school, first time at the dentist—first kiss, because somewhere behind you a grandma is applauding and encouraging your efforts.

After his first week in preschool, J told me he wasn't going back—ever.

"Why not?" I asked.

"Because I don't care for story circle," he said, "and everyone wants to kiss me."

"As you become clearer about who you really are, you'll be better able to decide what is best for you - the first time around."

~Oprah Winfrey quotes

Praying Hands

"Prayer does not change God but changes him who prays."
~Soren Kierkegaard

One of the classes in Making Words count for my young students talked about all the things we can do with our hands ... color, hold a book, write a story, hug ... and we can pray with our hands.

There's a picture of praying hands that hangs in our kitchen, one of the first paintings my mother did for me. Every time J see's that painting he has to fold his hands and pray.

If we forget to pray at meal times he folds his hands and shouts, "pray ... pray." No matter what type of prayer you say, be it the common table prayer, "Come Lord Jesus be our guest ..." or something straight from your heart you have to end it with "Thank you Jesus for this food ..." J's clue to say, "Amen."

If you add dessert to your plate be assured we'll pray again. Sometimes we pray two or three times, annoying to the adults in his life but pleasing to God. The little man loves to pray, a thrill to God's own heart—not to mention Grandma's! The value of prayer is to spend some personal time with God. Prayer is a lifeline to the Christian and the Jew. To pray is to talk to God.

Prayer is a personal act and can never be otherwise. To pray is to believe that there is someone listening who wants to hear those prayers. Prayer is only for those who believe that God is personal and wants a personal relationship with His creation. Both Christians and the Jew know the value of prayer as they both have encountered a God who declares "Talk to me and I shall listen."

Prayer provides power, poise, peace, and purpose—everything we want for our children and grandchildren. "Prayer is the prelude to peace, the prologue to power, the preface to purpose, and the pathway to perfection." Said William Arthur Ward an American college administrator (1921–1994).

Yes, prayer can and does make a difference. Not in the life of God, for He is complete and perfect, and, therefore, has no needs. But we have a need to transcend ourselves, to stand in awe before a mighty power. We have a need to recognize that there is something greater than ourselves, something to which we can aspire. As J's grandma I aspire, along with his parents and his Nana and Papa to help J get there to realize and depend upon the power of prayer. When J spends the night we do "goodnight prayers." It thrills my heart to hear him bless those he loves.

"What are you doing, J?" He was awfully quiet. "Are you thinking?"

"No Gamma, I praying."

"I was thinking of an old idea of self-discipline—an old Chinese proverb. He prayed every day—he had been taught to pray to our kind of God—and his prayer was, "Lord, reform Thy world, beginning with me."

~Franklin Delano Roosevelt

Dreams

"You see things and you say, "Why?" But I dream things that never were and say, "Why not?"
~George Bernard Shaw

Do babies dream? I wonder ... and if they do are their dreams of chasing butterflies perhaps, or throwing sticks for the dog to fetch ... dreaming of a new toy, or a new day? I suppose our existence could be considered to be "hum-drum" if it were not for our dreams.

"It may surprise you to know that it is thought children begin dreaming even before they are born. A large amount of Rapid Eye Movement sleep is required to stimulate the brain into action both before and after birth. We cannot know what a baby actually dreams about but we do know that children begin to talk about their dreams around the age of two years old. Toddlers will often dream about their daily lives, mothers, fathers, brothers, sisters and animals. A majority of two to three year olds actually associate dreaming with going to bed rather than going to sleep as we come to perceive it later on."
~From *Children's Dreams* by Jonathan Malory

In his book, *The DREAM Giver*, Bruce Wilkinson says that God is the dream giver. If you've ever read *"The Prayer of Jebes,"* of an Old Testament man who refused to settle for less. He cried out to God for larger borders, and for the power and protection to go with them. And God said, yes. If you pray like that, your life, as well, will change. In spite of the obstacles that may come your way, you can realize your dream and be all that God has destined you to be.

As Little J's grandma I hope to instill in him that sometimes he will have good dreams and sometimes he might have bad dreams, but to concentrate on the good dreams and to think about a different kind of dream— the kind of a dream that comes from the Dream Giver. And, just because

your little one wakes up screaming, do not assume it's because he's had a bad dream. It might just be that he's lost his place in his dream.
"Wow. Wow. Wow." J exclaimed upon coming into the kitchen. "I was dreaming on the way to your house that you would have cookies!"

I like to dream in red and blue.
I like to dream of me and you.
It's all I ever dream but then, I'm only two!

"A child awakened out of a deep sleep, expressed all the crying babies and all the weeping idealists in the world, "Oh, dear," he said. "I have lost my place in my dream."
~Lincoln Steffens

Patience

"Patience is the art of hoping."
~Vacvenargues

I always thought that God sent our cat King Tut into our lives to teach me patience and then I became a grandma. Becoming grandma in your 30's, 40's and 50's is one thing but to become a grandma for the first time in your 60's is another thing altogether. It kind of made me wonder what happened to my patience. From my book of "Unusual Quotations" I found this most interesting passage in regard to patience.

"Patience serves as a protection against wrongs, as clothes do against the cold. If you put on more clothes as the cold increases it will have no power to hurt you. So in a like manner you must grow in patience when you meet with wrong doings, exasperating circumstances or trying times. If you exercise patience these things you encounter along life's path will be powerless to vex your mind."
~Leonardo Da Vinci

Of all the qualities of an excellent character, shouldn't patience be enough? Well, unfortunately, in spite of the fact that it's one of the fruits of the spirit, it has never been my strong suite. I hoping it will be in J's favor as he grows from a toddler into a boy.

Do I see it yet? Not so much. He gets easily frustrated if he can't get the lid back on a jar, put a toy back together, fit the pieces into his puzzle—patience goes out the window. So how does one teach patience to a child?

J: Gamma I hungry.
Grandma: I'm making lunch as fast as I can.
J: Faster Gamma, I hungry a lot.

When waiting in line with her 4-year-old twin girls Anna and Josie, Jennifer Miller, a Maryland-based mom, has her own special way of refocusing her girls' attention. "Whether it's waiting in line or waiting for dinner, I just refocus their attention on something else. Distraction can be a very useful tool with young children," Miller says. She already sees evidence that her girls are beginning to learn to entertain themselves. "Sure, they still whine when they have to wait for something," Miller admits. "But more and more, I see them automatically turning their attention where they know I'll be directing it anyway."

> Grandma: J maybe you could color while I make lunch.
> J: I don't think I can.
> Grandma: Why not?
> J: My hungry doesn't like to color.

The Waiting is the Hardest Part ... waiting to go to the store, or to Grandma's house or harder yet, waiting for Christmas—all of which take forever when you are just a kid. As Tom Petty croons in one of his songs, in this hurry up and wait society, the waiting is indeed the hardest part. Children would love nothing more than the hours and minutes between now and when a vacation or plate of spaghetti would materialize. Therefore, patience is a key to success.

Self-control and patience are important if kids are going to succeed in school as well as life after school, so the sooner they learn it the better. And it's our job as parents and grandparents to give our kids that start.

"Successfully teaching patience is more than just teaching your children to wait," says Corinne Gregory, founder and president of Social Smarts, a nationally recognized program of teaching social skills, character and values to kids. "It also means teaching them how to be willing to wait calmly, particularly in the face of delay.

If you really want to try your patience, volunteer to take my daughter's dog for a weekend. He'll definitely teach you the value of patience. If that fails practice shuffling cards. Patience and shuffling cards seem to go together at least they do for me and especially if I'm playing cards with Jeremiah.

"Gamma, don't play with the cards ... just mix 'em all up, please."

I'm getting older now. I have a lot more aches and pains. I especially notice them after a day chasing the little man around. With these aches I've learned to be grateful. In old age patience is everything.

"A man who is the master of patience is the master of everything."
~Lord Halifax

Any Questions?

"It's better to ask some of the questions then to know all the answers."
~James Thurber

J is talking now, it happened a little over two years of age. I suspect now that he's putting words together it's only the beginning. Am I ready for the questions? The following are real questions ask by children of various ages. (And a few questions of my own lol)

Grandma, why are you so fluffy?

Why is Grandpa's head growing through his hair?

Why is it that people say they "slept like a baby" when babies wake up like every two hours?

What do you mean I eat like a bird? Birds don't like broccoli, do they?

Why are you IN a movie, but you're ON TV?

Why do people pay to go up tall buildings and then put money in binoculars to look at things on the ground?

If a deaf person has to go to court, is it still called a hearing?

Why do Buffalo wings taste like chicken?

Why is it that no matter what color bubble bath you use the bubbles are always clear?

Why do spiders look the way they do?

Why can't I get a pet monkey? I have money.

Why can't cars fly like airplanes?

Why does Grandma make funny noises when she sleeps?

If a cow laughed hard, would milk come out of her nose?

Do brown cows make chocolate milk?

Why does a round pizza come in a square box?

Why do people who know the least know it the loudest?

What do you call a male ladybug?

What hair color do they put on the driver's license of a bald man?

If you choke a Smurf, what color does it turn?

What color is a chameleon on a mirror?

Grandma, have you ever seen a toad on a toadstool?

Grandma, did I come from a monkey or from God?

Grandma I don't like mosquitoes. Why didn't Noah swat those two mosquitoes?

Why do we say "Something is out of whack"? What is a whack, anyway?

I can't wait for little J to start asking; I think I'm ready for his questions.

J: Gamma I want to come to your house ... when can I come to your house, Gamma?

Grandma: Maybe tomorrow.

J: Is that very long?

J: Gamma, I'm going to be bad today.

Grandma: Why?

J: Because I want to be bad.

Grandma: Then you'll have to go to time out.

J: Oh well, I'm still going to be bad today.

"The 'silly question' is the first intimation of some totally new developments."

~Alfred North Whiteman

Rules

"There never was a rule that didn't have to be broken at some time and a man who didn't know when to break a rule is a fearful pain in the neck."

~William Feather

Bishop William Stubbs had only three rules of life he followed: Never do anything underhanded. Never get your feet wet. Go to bed at ten. For the average man a sufficient rule of life, according to W. Maugham, (*Book of Unusual Quotations*) is to follow your instincts.

J is only two; he's just learning about life and its rules. I think as parents and grandparents, with each generation, we have to learn life's rules all over again ourselves. In a sense Grandpa and Grandma are learning how to follow the rules, too. I don't envy parents today as they struggle through the process of guiding and teaching their children to have acceptable behavior within certain limits, to cooperate, to be responsible, and to think for themselves.

Rules and discipline seem to go hand in hand. **Discipline** is not the same as **punishment**. **Punishment** treats the person as wrong and deals with the past. **Discipline** treats the **act** as wrong and deals with the present and what should happen in the future. The goal for children is to gradually gain an inner sense of self-discipline that will guide them in the world. **Different ages and stages of development present different needs and discipline challenges:**

— **Age one:** Little J throws his Cheerios on the floor. "Don't do that, baby," I say. He just smiles. Silly, Grandma, the little man cannot understand and follow rules yet, but he's learning that he can't always behave as he pleases.

— **Age two:** Grandma reads J a book. J throws the book on the floor when we're done.

"Jeremiah, we pick up our books and put them back on the shelve." Jeremiah smiles. Grandma is so proud he's beginning to follow simple rules. Then he throws all the books off the shelf—what fun! OK, so he's not able, yet, to follow rules consistently, but we'll get there.

— **Age three**: J comes to Grandma's ... first thing he does is dump all his toys on the floor. Grandma insists that he picks up his tools before we get out the records. J looks at gamma with raised eyebrows ... it takes a lot of prodding but he does it. "Yeah. Good job." He can follow a few more rules now; he's not always consistent because it's tough being consistent when you're only three. It's tough for Grandma to enforce the rules when he smiles at me and says, "Gamma, you are my bestest friend."

Enforcing rules—isn't that a parents job? Yes and J's parents are doing a darn good job. J typically comes when called, waits for his turn, avoids most dangers, and obeys the adults in charge. Wait a minute ... maybe that's the dog?

— **Age four**: We're not there, yet, but I'm looking forward to it. I suspect my precious genius will still only have limited self-control but heck, how hard can turning four be? The little man is growing up; he already follows directions, obeys authority figures, (most of the time) return things to their proper place, (some of the time) and treats things with care, at least when he's at Grandma's house. Setting up rules (and consequences) wasn't that hard. Thanks, Matt and Amanda—you've done a great job so far! As for Grandma, maybe when it comes to "spoiling" she needs a little time out. But if you're patient she'll get it right.

If you're a parent (or grandparent) reading this and you are struggle with rules—the following may help:

1. Decide on the rules needed to protect the family.

2. Rules are in place to promote fairness in the home. Children under age five are not motivated to follow rules in order to do what is right yet. They act more to gain approval from the important adults in their lives or to avoid consequences.

3. Create your family rules. Hang the rules for everyone to see. If your child is old enough (4 or over), allow them to help you create the rules list.

4. Determine appropriate consequences for breaking each rule; make sure the consequences fit your individual child and are age appropriate. It's most important, even for grandparents to be firm and immediate with the consequences.

5. Be firm and consistent with consequences established for breaking the rules. Knowing right from wrong is an abstract concept that takes time and experience to understand. So give your child the time he needs to experience life, including life's rules.

6. Change the rules as your child "outgrows" them, when his/her behavior becomes normal for his/her age.

Rules even for adults are not always easy to follow. So remember, parents and grandparents, praise your children when they follow the rules. Ultimately, we are all teaching our children that acting out or doing something that's inappropriate have consequences. "Naughty" = time out. "Being good, showing good behavior" = good results which equals good rewards.

So as grandparents if we are going to help parents establish rules then we ought to know life's rules ourselves. So grandma's and grandpa's, here are 10 rules for you to live by: (And help you cope with being grandparents. lol)

1. Learn to relax around your grandchildren. Don't let them get the better of you.

2. Love your bed, it is your temple—and you'll want to go there as soon as the little ones leave!

3. If your children drop off the kids and the dog—relax, stand, sit or lay down beside them! You'll become great friends.

4. Relax in the day, so that you can sleep at night! (Especially if the grandkids are on a sleepover at your house.)

5. Work is holy, so don't attack it, especially when the grandkids come over just forget work altogether!

6. Don't do something today or tomorrow, (for that matter) that you can do the day afterwards! Enjoy your little ones!

7. In fact, dear ones—you're retired now so work as little as possible. Let others do what needs to be done! Your job is to be grandma/grandpa!

8. Don't worry, nobody ever died from doing nothing, but you could get hurt at work! Come to think about it you could get hurt wrestling with the grandson! If that should happen go back to rule #2.

9. If you feel like doing work, sit down and wait until that feeling goes away!

10. Don't forget: working is healthy! So leave it for the sick people!

Now that you have the rules memorized—go be grandparents!

"The young man knows the rules but the old man knows the exceptions."
~Oliver Wendell Holmes

Goodnight Nobody

"One of the greatest diseases is to be nobody to anybody."
~Mother Teresa

If you're wondering why this page is mostly blank, it's because J's favorite page in the book, *Goodnight Moon* is the blank page that simply says, "Goodnight nobody." He likes to shout that out before I even turn the page.

But God makes no mistakes and everybody is somebody. So this page is blank—half time, if you will. Time to give your precious babe a marker and let him draw something of his own design. It will be your favorite page in this book, guaranteed.

Games with Clouds

"There are no rules of architecture for a castle in the clouds."
~G. K. Chesterton quotes

I started writing poems, songs and stories for my kids as soon as they were born. Those stories were sadly put away when they grew up. So you can imagine how excited I was when Little J was born to pull out those stories again. And, I found myself writing new stories and songs for the little man. One of my favorites, "Lookin' at Clouds."

Lookin' at Clouds
By Connie Hawkins

I like to lie on the ground
And look up at the clouds
The things I see they tickle me
And make me laugh out loud

Oh look—there's goes an elephant
Walking on his ele- trunk
Followed by a big red moose
Followed by a skunk

Is that a … fountain or a mountain?
A duck, a boat—a goose
It's hard to tell just what I see
When the clouds are laughing back at me …

I can't wait for the day when I can sit on the grass with the little man and teach him cloud games and fun, happy songs. Maybe we'll even make up songs together … like, "I love my grandma and my grandma loves me … Ya Ya Ya …" the rest of the words will come in time. Ask him about "Heidi

Didi Doo lost her favorite shoe ..." He knows Grandma makes up silly songs and he loves it just like his daddy did.

"Life exists for the love of music or beautiful things."
~G. K. Chesterton quotes

What's in a Name?

"What's in a name? That which we call a rose by any other name would smell as sweet."

~Shakespeare

JEREMIAH

Gender: Masculine

Usage: English, Biblical

Other Scripts: וְהִיָמְרִי (Ancient Hebrew)

Pronounced: jer-ə-MIE-ə (English)

From the Hebrew name וְהִיָמְרִי (*Yirmiyahu*) which meant "YAHWEH has uplifted." This was the name of one of the major prophets of the Old Testament, author of the Book of Jeremiah and (supposedly) the Book of Lamentations. He lived to see the Babylonian destruction of Jerusalem in the 6th century BC. In England though the vernacular form *Jeremy* had been occasionally used since the 13th century, the form *Jeremiah* was not common until after the Protestant Reformation.

Good old apple pie and baseball are just some of the hallmarks of American culture. Capture a bit of the essence of the pure American spirit in your baby's name. There is so much more to Jack and Sue than meets the eye.

At a lost for names, or simply bored with common names, parents began naming their kids after movie stars, characters from a movie or TV show, song titles, something out of a poem or book—even the weather … i.e. Sunny Day, Stormy. Star, Brooke.

American pop culture influences baby name choices not only in the States, but in Europe, Asia and other remote regions. A writer's decision for a character name on a TV show can have lasting effects on a whole generation. Take the soap opera *Days of Our Lives* for example. A character named Kayla gave the name incredible popularity, and hundreds if not thousands of Kayla's today are the product of the show's trendsetting influence.

A similar phenomenon can be seen in the UK. The name Keira, and its alternative spelling Kiera, jumped up in popularity when British actress Keira Knightly became famous worldwide for her roles in *Bend It Like Beckham* and *Pirates of the Caribbean.* Even a bad reputation has been known to spark trends. An evil nanny named Peyton in the film *The Hand that Rocks the Cradle* made the name an instant favorite, whereas before it was virtually unheard of *(Internet article)*

Today, names like Tyler, Trenton, Ryder, Brianna or Bre have taken the lead in popular names for kids. The Bible says, "A good name is to be more desired than great riches …" ~Proverbs 22:1 And so we have our Jeremiah, Hebrew for "uplifted."

Ask him what his name is and he'll say, "Jermina or Jer-my-ia." I just love this little man. Later, it was Jeremiah Pat after Pat Sajak (No, Pat is not the little man's middle name. You'll read that story later.)

"Any child can tell you that the sole purpose of a middle name is so
he can tell when he's really in trouble."
~Dennis Frakes

Noise

"A baby is a loud noise at one end and no sense of responsibility at
the other."
~Ronald Knox

Some would describe a boy as "noise" with dirt on his face. And, Little
J can make his share of noise whether he's simply talking or banging on
the piano, running or jumping—even sitting to read a book—noise comes.
But what exactly is noise? The official definition of "noise" according to
Webster's Dictionary is, any unwanted sound; a loud and/or unpleasant
sound.

Noise music is a term used to describe varieties of avant-garde music
and sound art that may use elements such as cacophony, dissonance, ato-
nality, **noise**, indeterminacy, and repetition.

The word noise, pronounced "no iz." The etymology of noise is Middle
English; from early French noise "quarrel, loud noise," from the Latin,
nausea "seasickness, nausea" derived from Greek nautes "sailor." 1: a loud,
confused, or senseless shouting or outcry. 2: a sound, especially a loud,
harsh, or unharmonious sound.

Word History Although loud noises may make us sick, we probably do
not think of the words *noise* and *nausea* as having much in common. But
the word *noise* came into English from early French, in which it meant
"quarrel, loud noise." French had it from the Latin word *nausea* meaning "seasickness, nausea." Perhaps the original connection was with the
unpleasant sounds or complaints made by seasick passengers or sailors.
Nausea, after all, came from the Greek word for sailor, *nautēs*.

The world's notables have it all wrong—noise is simply a boy in motion.

No matter the technical definition of noise—it truly is, as far as this
grandma is concerned, a boy with dirt on his face. And, there are a million noises for a boy with dirt on his face to enjoy from sound machines
to music machines. Our Little J is fascinated with the sound that "things"
make, the clang that comes when you crash to glasses together, the bang

of candle sticks hitting one another. What happens when you hit a spoon against the register, ah, thus comes a new way to play a drum! Hitting your hands against the coffee table makes a different sound and vibration then hitting the footstool. Scratching your fingers across the window pane, ouch; blowing into a straw or a horn is fun. Dragging chalk across a blackboard—not so fun. I vote for clapping our hands and stomping our feet—that's enough noise for any day!

J: Gamma do stars make noise?
Grandma: I think stars twinkle.
J: Oh … I like noisy stars better.

"Everybody has their taste in noises as well as in other matters."
~Joseph Addison

By the way, "The stars make no noise"
~Irish Sayings quotes

Funny Faces

"I practiced making faces in the mirror and it would drive my mother crazy. She used to scare me by saying that I was going to see the devil if I kept looking in the mirror. That fascinated me even more, of course."

~Jim Carrey

I think most people naturally have a beautiful face and even a face that may not seem beautiful is beautiful to a mother. I thought my children were beautiful babies and my grandchildren—no doubt are beautiful.

What makes a beautiful face? Expressive eyes, a perfect little nose. Delicate ears, lips that purse just right—and a head of curly hair to define all those features. When I was a kid growing up on the farm, I did not consider myself a beautiful child—I was anything but. I didn't like my hair, my body or my personality and I definitely hated the way that I walked. Mom would tell me there was always someone worse off then me—that everyone had flaws. She was right. Our neighbor only had one eye; his father had a goiter. The butcher was old with more wrinkles on his face then you could shake a stick at. My cousin said her nose was too big and a kid in my school had floppy ears. What do you do when you're thinking of all your imperfections? That's easy: Make faces!

Little J has a million faces. Somehow, right from the cradle, he knew that his faces were entertaining. The more we would laugh the more faces he would make.

There's the angry eyebrows he raises when he's unhappy about something.

There's his "posing for the camera" face with big round eyes or lips pursed as he shouts, "Cheese."

There's the "I don't want to face" he makes when it's time to take a nap and he'd rather do something else.

There's the ice cream face, the dirty face, the happy, clown face and the "I don't want to talk to you face."

But the face I love the best and I'm sure his mom does, too, is the sweet little cherub face of a sleeping boy.

J: Gamma, is this a smile?" J turns a pouty face to me.
Grandma: "Yes," I said, "but it's turned upside down."

There's nothing more wonderful then sweet baby faces and the smiles and giggles they insure. I'd walk a million miles for one of J's smiles!

"I like bringing smiles to people's faces."
~Jai Rodriguez

Possibility

"A new baby is like the beginning of all things - wonder, hope, a dream of possibilities."

~Eda J. Le Shan

When Little J was born I saw all the above, wonder, hope and a multitude of possibilities. If we handled it right, this kid could grow up to be anything and everything. One thing that was clear from the start was his love to make music. He was standing at his Fisher Price music maker testing out the sounds it made long before he should have been. We tried taking it apart once to sit it on the floor so it would be easier for him to use, (Grandma got tired of holding him up) but that idea was short-lived. The little man preferred to stand when he danced!

He was interested in sound—the sound of water running; the sounds that came out of his drum, things that talked and made music, doors opening and closing, things that squeaked—sound was music to J. The fact that he had a sound machine running at night probably helped to spark this curiosity in sound. I could see a promising rock star, singer, song writer—even a dancer. Put a baton in his hands—who knows he could end up taking over as musical director in church one day. (Sorry Pastor Leon) Give him a microphone … I could go on and on. Achievable goals are endless.

Okay, Okay … maybe a basketball star or a brain surgeon or a writer like his Grandma Connie. Doesn't matter what's in my mind or anyone else's for that matter; God has a plan for the course of J's life.

J's just beginning. He has the whole world at his finger tips.

"Gamma, I think you would like a pano concert." J pulls me into the living room. "You can sit here," he points to the couch. "I play pano for you."

"In the beginner's mind there are many possibilities, in the expert's mind there are few."

~Shunryu Suzuki

"In short, we cannot grow, we cannot achieve authentic discovery, and our eyes cannot be cleansed to the truly beautiful possibilities of life, if we simply live a neutral existence."

~Armstrong Williams

The Senses

"Live with all of your senses."
~Sue Townsend

One of the classes taught in my "Making Words Count" writing workshops for kids involved writing with the senses, how taste, smell, sound and sight, play an important part in writing. In fact, you really can't write without involving the senses.

Hans Hofmann (BrainyQuotes) wrote that "A work of art is a world in itself reflecting senses and emotions of the artist's world." This is true for artists, painters, writers, actors and for children learning what the senses are all about.

"Beauty must appeal to the senses, must provide us with immediate enjoyment, must impress us or insinuate itself into us without any effort on our part."
~Claude Debussy

It would be with great love that I would teach the little man about the important part that his senses would play in his discoveries, but as an author I am particularly drawn to teaching J the importance of writing with the senses. Oh, what fun we had in those classes, introducing different smells, i.e. vinegar, nail polish remover, powder, watching the kids trying to figure out what their nose was telling them. Closing our eyes and listening to the sound of a woodpecker, a train whistle—crinkling tinfoil. "Listen and write," I would instruct. Things to touch and things to taste; there was never a dull moment in our writing with the senses classes.

I can't wait to do a mini session with my grandchildren (notice I said grandchildren), sticking cotton balls, feathers and buttons on construction paper; tasting a lemon and comparing that to ice cream!

Yep, Little J and I are going to have a fine time with the senses, pending Grandma doesn't come to her senses, first!

J: "Gamma, know what this is?"

Grandma: "Yes," I answer, "It's a cotton ball and I'm going to tickle you with it."

J: "Gamma, know what this is?"

Grandma: "Yes, Little J, it's a sucker."

J: "I gonna eat it!"

"Love is the poetry of the senses."

~Honore de Balzac

Stubborn

"A man will do more for his stubbornness than for his religion or his country."

~E. W. Howe

As children, we can be stubborn and say we get it from our mothers or bull-headed like our fathers, or have a bit of temper like Grandpa. We grow up set in our ways and blame it on our forefathers—what's new? This has been the plague of parenthood down through the ages. So what's a new born to do? What chance do they stand?

Personally, I think character flaws (and we all have them) should be down played as much as possible and a lifestyle of stubbornness/bull-headedness should attract as little or no attention at all—if doable. Remember all things are possible in Christ.

I admit I can be as stubborn as they come, but I am also passionate and reasonable (I think). My mother was passionate about things she believed in; she was also stubborn and bossy. (I call it facilitating). Am I like my mother—you bet I am!

Is Little J stubborn? Sometimes. Can he be bull-headed? He has his moments. Does he show his temper? He can. He is strong-willed? You bet he is.

I think we are all in bondage to our personality and character flaws—be those good or bad. "Bondage is the life of personality, and for bondage the personal self will fight with tireless resourcefulness and the most stubborn cunning." ~Aldous Huxley. It's part of life, part of who we are. No one can escape it.

Gregory Peck said in a TV interview once, "I had that stubborn streak, it's the Irish in me, I guess." I guess maybe we're all a little Irish now and then. I'm not picking on the Irish; the French, the Polish, the Italians can have that same stubborn streak in them. Stubborn shows no mercy to gender, nationality or origin. "So, as one sees, I by no means deprive my world of stubborn reality, if I merely call it a world of ideas." ~Josiah Royce. My applause goes to Josiah Royce.

As J turns into a delightful three year old, we hear a lot of: "I can do it myself." And I believe he will.

"Gamma, look what I can do?" Painting on the wall, not a good idea. "I did it all by myself, Gamma." Gamma went out and bought a very large paint book and now we paint together—on paper!

"Many are stubborn in pursuit of the path they have chosen, few in pursuit of the goal."
~Friedrich Nietzsche

Sunday School is Fun

"Mom and Dad would stay in bed on Sunday morning, but the kids would have to go to church."

~Lynn Johnston

I wonder when Little J grows up if he'll have a great testimony of salvation. If he'll speak of how his parents took him to church every Sunday? I am confident that he will. He already loves to go to church.

I am thankful that I came from a Christian family, that my parents when to church every Sunday and took me to Sunday School where I learned about the things of God and heard great Bible stories, like Noah and the Ark, and Moses on the mountain. I learned the Lord's Prayer, the Beatitudes and the books of the Bible in the Presbyterian Church. I accepted Jesus Christ as my personal savior when I was 13 years old and have not wavier in my walk.

The little man grew restless in the nursery and was happy to go into the toddler class; there were big boy toys and other kids to play with and songs to sing and prayers to pray. Sometimes he'd go in unhappy but always came out smiling. Hopefully, this excitement will continue as he advances from class to class, from story to story, from scripture to scripture.

One Sunday he came bouncing out of his class with a paper plate folded in half and glued together with multi-colored streamers hanging and I assumed beans or rice inside. On the outside was a scribbling of colors.

"Wow," I marveled. "What did you make in Sunday School?"

"It's a Taco," J said.

Grandma smiled. I was so proud.

The second Sunday in Wonder Church (the 3-year old class) he had glued clouds on a piece of paper with a scripture verse written on the paper. "Wow, look at those clouds—they are beautiful." I exclaimed.

"Gamma," he looked up me with an expression of complete amazement, "its cotton." Like, I should know the difference between cotton and clouds. Kids, don't you just love 'em!

"Train up a child in the way that he should go and when he is old he will not depart from it."
~Proverbs 22:6

Relatives

"Every family has prize kin."
~E.W. Howe

When Little J was born, all the relatives came one by one to see him (and friends, as well) to usher this new life into the family. He was the star quarterback–the new family member. And the family—all his relatives oohed and aahed over what a marvel he was.

The definition of family:
The collective body of persons who live in one house, and under one head or manager; a household, including parents, children, and servants, and, as the case may be, lodgers or boarders.

A group, comprising a husband and wife and their dependent children, constituting a fundamental unit in the organization of society.

Those who descend from one common progenitor; a tribe, clan, or race; kindred; house; as, the human family; the family of Abraham; the father of a family.

Course of descent; genealogy; line of ancestors; lineage.

Honorable descent; noble or respectable stock; as, a man of family.

A group of kindred or closely related individuals; as, a family of languages; a family of States; the chlorine family—the relatives, if you will.

We don't have control over the kind of a family we are born into. I remember as a girl, I always wanted to be part of my friend Mary's family. And likewise, she wanted to live with my family. I think all kids go through that at some time or another. Little J is only two, but he knows when he wants to go to Grandma's or Nana's house. Already, he likes to spend the night. By the time he was three, he was requesting more frequent visits—like every day!

Relativity speaking, relatives are fun, with exception of nighttime prayers when one must go through the blessing of the relatives. As the little man grows so grows his list of blessings. I hope he continues to count his family as blessings, and that he will grow up to cherish his family, to appreciate his heritage.

George Bernard Shaw said of family, "A happy family is but an earlier heaven." In other words, you should be happy in your family as you will be in heaven. But my favorite quote comes from Michael J Fox. "Family is not an important thing, it's everything." Even in her royalty, Princess Diana said that, "Family is the most important thing in the world."

In spite of the fact that you may have a family tree in need of a good trimming, cherish your family because truer words were never spoken, family is the most important thing in the world and I'm so glad that Little J is part of our family and that together we are a part of the family of God.

One day, Little J had the shoe house out and the little people that lived in the shoe lined up one by one. "This is the mommy and this is the daddy," he explained to me. "And these are all the children."

"Wow, that's a lot of children," I said.

"So many children," he said. "I will take them to K-Mart." He proceeded to load them into the back of his dump truck and dumped them off at K-Mart. "Someone will buy them."

"But, don't you want them?"

"They're not mine, Gamma, they yours."

"If you raise your children to feel that they can accomplish any goal or task they decide upon, you will have succeeded as a parent and you will have given your children the greatest of all blessings."
    ~Brian Tracy

Right and Wrong

"No one knows what he is doing while he acts right, but of what is wrong we are always Conscious."
~Goethe

I'm only two what do I know of right and wrong of black from blue.
I cannot cook or tie my shoe. Is that wrong? Not when you're only two.
Right or wrong, red or green—the world's crazy so it seems.

Don't climb on the table; don't mess with the cable …
Stop pulling the dogs tail—no loud songs
All of these things must be wrong.

Right and wrong, black and white
Mama smiles when I sing
Singing must be right.

"When a man is old enough to do wrong, he should be old enough to Do right, also."
~Oscar Wilde

I love watching J while he's learning … right shoe on the left foot, shirt on inside out. He knows what he wants to wear and when he wants to wear it. Trying to convince him that he can't wear his beach shoes to church on Sunday (not to be confused with his crocks, which he loves to wear anytime) or that you wear your winter coat when its cold out doesn't fly with Jeremiah.

He already has his favorite jeans and insists that Grandma wear her jeans when he's wearing his, and especially when we are wrestling. Apparently, we can only wrestle in our jeans. And we need to wear our comfy pants when we nap. And Grandma should wear only her gray tennis shoes not her black ones and we take our church pants off if we are going outside to play. I have much to learn about what's right and what isn't.

"Confidence comes not from always being right but from not fearing to be wrong."

~Peter T. Mcintyre

Hats

"With the right hat, nothing else matters."
~LaPaloma Hats

Grandpa has so many hats—"So many hats and only one head."
~Author unknown

J's fascination with hats lives on. What's a little man to do? But wear hats, too. Like his grandpa, J has had his share of hats—he doesn't always wear them but he sure seems to enjoy at least the idea of having a hat.

Why is it that kids love hats? They like to make them, wear them, throw them and lose them! My kids could never find their winter caps and gloves; it seemed like every snow season I was out looking for new hats, gloves and scarfs. J's Mama seems to have the same problem with sun hats for the little man; he has a variety of them along with caps, never to be found when you really need one.

"When a man buys a new hat he wants one just the like he has had before. But a woman isn't that way."
~E.W. Howe

Baseball caps and hunting hats
Summer hats made out of straw
And winter wool for winter's thaw
Hats to wear on a boat, on a horse on a goat
Hats you wear to chit and chat
Grandpa has a lot of hats!

Grandma helped me make a hat
With a little of this and a little of that
With lots of ribbons and a bow
I didn't like it very much it was too pink for me
So I took that silly little hat
And gave it to my cat!

"Never run after your own hat—others will be delighted to do it for
you; Why spoil their fun."
~Mark Twain

Snow

"Snow and adolescence are the only problems that disappear if you ignore them long enough."
~Earl Wilson quotes

All bundled up in a snowsuit three sizes to big for him, I wasn't sure if that was the little man coming down the walk or an alien! I'm not quite sure what was going through J's mind upon that first snow fall, what he was thinking when his daddy handed him a shovel! Ah, good job, Dad, he'll get it, hopefully by the time he's twelve!

Goethe said of snow, "Snow is fake cleanliness."

Fake or not, snow seems to cleanse and make the world look new and hopeful. There's something special about that first snow fall—it's even more special when a baby sees it for the first time. The look of merriment that dances in their eyes as they reach out to catch a snowflake.

When it snows, you have two choices. You can complain about having to shovel it, or you can play in it! Both children and adults prefer the latter. One fires up the snowmobile, the other fires up his imagination creating snowmen, snow forts and snow angels.

When you're a child, the first snow fall is a sight to behold—it is in every sense of the word magical. And kids don't seem to mind the snow that blows against their cheek or freezes on their eyelashes. They don't mind bundling up and going out to play in all that fluff. Moms don't mind either, until they hear that little one say, "I gots to go potty." Off come the gloves, the boots the snow pants. How well I remember those days.

My favorite snow story involves a friends daughter who was going outside in the middle of June with a canister filled with flour in one hand and a bottle of water in the other hand—to make snow, she told her mother.

"Gamma, do you have any gloves I can wear?"

"Why?" I asked. "Its summer, it's not time for snow."

"I just want to be ready."

"To appreciate the beauty of a snow flake, it is necessary to stand out in the cold."

~Author unknown

The Telephone

"America's best buy is a telephone call to the right man."
~Ilka Chase

Grandmas are silly people who will hold the phone up to their ear and listen to baby babbles and gurgles as if it were intelligent conversation. And eventually it is.

The little man loves to talk on the telephone. I love it when J gets on the phone, "Hello, Gamma … .babble gurgle … toys … fun. Bye bye." I'm in seventh heaven for days.

I don't think parents realize how special grandchildren really are; they cannot possibly understand that until they themselves become grandparents.

To be a grandma is a lot different then being a mom … because, well, because we have time to be silly, time to play games, like "monkey on my back" sing songs, take walks and talk on the telephone. We have time to ask our grandchildren about their day and what did they do that was fun on a rainy afternoon.

People who have no time to sit around and wait for the telephone to ring obviously have no grandchildren

I'll tell you just how smart J is … he has the numbers on my cell phone figured out. He knows which one to push to call Pa.

One day he got a hold of his father's phone and called me … the phone rang, I picked it up, said "hello" and heard babbling on the other end. He's done that a couple of times. I told his Dad, "You'd better be careful, one of these days he'll call Japan and you'll get the bill!"

Ring. Ring. "Hello …"

"Gamma, come over." Click.

That's my little man!

"The bathtub was invented in 1850 and the telephone in 1875. In other words, if you had been living in 1850, you could have sat in the bathtub for 25 years without having to answer the phone."
~Bill DeWitt, 1972

Love of God

"Live to seek God and life will not be without God."
~Leo Tolstroy

We are all on the same page when it comes to teaching Little J about the love of God. I was raised in a Christian home; spiritual values were instilled in me at an early age. When children learn God's truths early, they can grow spiritually and have the wonderful life that God has planned for them. I am so thankful that my children are teaching their children about God's love. This will bring honor and glory to our Lord and an opportunity for the children to have inner happiness and contentment in life.

Little J is on God's team. There is joy in watching him praise the Lord, clapping his hands during praise and worship and sometimes reminding the adults in his life to pray.

When God is part of life in the cradle He will be present at their table, in their home and in their lives.

Questions kids ask God:
Why did you make my grandpa so old?
Could you tell my little brother it's not nice to bite?
Why do I have to go to school? Couldn't you just make me smart?
Why did you send me a sister when I wanted a dog?
Why do I have to wear underwear?
Where is Mass-a-chutes?
Do the angels sleep at night?
God if you made everything, who made you?
God does Jesus like baseball?
Why are girls so crabby all the time?
When I die will I live with you or Jesus?

"The foundation of all foundations, the pillar supporting all wisdom, is the recognition of the reality of God."
~Moses Maimonides (From the *Book of Unusual Quotations*)

Moms and Dads

"It is not possible for one to teach others if one cannot teach his own family."
~Confucius

Mom and Dad were the first people that Little J saw when he opened his eyes. His family at that moment in time was Mom and Dad. Mom's and dad's play the most important role in a little one's life; they are the ones, with God's help, who will mold and shape and create.

"When I was a boy of fourteen, my father was so ignorant I could hardly stand to have the old man around, but when I got to be twenty-one I was astonished at how much he had learned in seven years!"
~Mark Twain

I think most of us go through life thinking our parents don't know a whole lot; we wish we had different parents, wiser, kinder, and richer and sometimes you might even hear kids say, "I wish my parents were stricter."

Tough love is the key to raising successful children. Parents are not in place to befriend, to create laughter, to go along with the crowd. They are to guide and to nurture, to discipline and to teach. Little J will have plenty of friends but only one mom and dad. His mother is the first women he'll ever love and his dad the first man he'll look up.

A Little Fellow Follows Me

A careful man I ought to be,
A little fellow follows me.
I dare not go astray,
For fear he'll go the self-same way.

I cannot once escape his eyes,
Whatever he see me do, he tries.
Like me, he says, he's going to be,
The little chap who follows me.

He thinks that I am good and fine,
Believes in every word of mine.
The base in me he must not see,
That little fellow who follows me.

I must remember as I go,
Thru summers' sun and winters' snow.
I am building for the years to be,
In the little chap who follows me.

By Rev. Claude Wisdom White, Sr

Need I say more?

Jack's Place and Cows

"Friendship increases in visiting friends, but in visiting them seldom."
  ~Sir Francis Bacon Sr

I have to disagree with Francis Bacon. I think one should visit their friends and family often so the pathway to their door doesn't become choked with weeds. And so, I take Little J to Jack's place to visit his Great-Grandpa Willis. My father is in a foster care home and Jack is his care taker. I've taken J to see Grandpa since he was old enough to walk.

The first time I took him, I thought he might be afraid but that was not the case; he walked in as if to say, "Here I am." Paid no never mind to Grandpa but strutted through the place as if he owned it, investigating every kook and cranny, visiting every room.

"Say hello to Jack," I said, "and give Grandpa Willis a hug."

Not sure which one of these old men living in Jack's house was "grandpa" they all got hugs, including Jack who was busy doing the laundry and really didn't need J's help, but J being blessed with the gift of "help" pitched right in putting socks into the dryer and helping Jack to fold the towels.

But the thing that really attracts the little man to Jack's place is Jack's collection of cows, especially the laughing cow. Now what a sight that is to see the little man showing the old men how to laugh. It was months later that J discovered the penny cow—he'd ask Jack for a penny so he could put it in the cow and hear it moo.

Not to long ago when we were visiting, J discovered that Jack had donkeys in his back yard and horses. "Those are burrows," Jack informed us. Donkeys or burrows they were all horses to J and he couldn't wait to go outside to see them. They come right up to the fence and will let you pet them. Luckily, Pa was with us that day so he could take Little J out to play.

Along with four residents, there's also a cat named Molly, who like J's cat, Jinx, runs to hide whenever Little J's around.

One of my fondest memories is Little J climbing up into Grandpa Willis' chair to give him a hug. It will be forever etched in my mind.

Hugs and kisses to everyone J will return.

Note: Grandpa Willis died November 11, 2011. At the funeral home, J
said "We should be quiet … Grandpa is sleeping in a box." Rest in peace
Granddad.

> "Visits always give pleasure, if the not the coming then the going!"
> ~From *Apples of Gold*

Bully or Bullied?

"A wise man thinks its better not to enter the fight then to win."
~LaRochefougauld

For Father's Day, 2011, I thought a picnic at the park would be perfect. The adults would have space to sit and relax, the dog would have room to run and Little J could play on the playground.

Most parks have assorted playground equipment, some specifically designed for toddlers and others for older kids. Of course we took J to the toddler area where he could climb and swing and slide. He was easily bored with that and wanted to go down the big boy slide; there he sat at the top of the slide ready to go and down he went with a swoosh. Grandpa was there to catch him and Grandma there to applaud. I was a little bit nervous watching him climb—it seemed so high up and the sign definitely said: Ages 5 and over. J was only 2+ but determined to master the monkey bars.

Then it was on to another play area with a play house and more monkey bars and ladders to climb. He was particularly fascinated by the inside of the whales belly and took several minutes climbing through it.

"Move!" a little boy about 5 shouted as he came up behind J. "Move little boy it's my turn now."

J did the only thing he could. He turned around and pushed the boy.

"Trouble on the playground," I shouted to J's mama who came running.

"Is it J, is he hurt?"

"Yes, it's J, but no, he's not hurt."

"That baby pushed me." The older boy sobbed to his mother.

I had all I could do to keep from laughing. Bully or bullied? I don't think we are going to have to worry about Little J making his way through life!

"The only way to settle a disagreement is on the basis of what's right—
not who's right."
~Apples of Gold

Don't Mess With My Stuff

"The things you own end up owning you."
~Tyler Durden quotes

It didn't take long for me to learn that the little man doesn't like change. First, I changed my bedroom around. He was quick to point out that I had the bed in the wrong spot—it goes against the wall—not the window. When he was about 1½, I dropped the cord to the light behind the bed and broke it. Pa had to fix it. Now, J's two and a half and he still talks about that broken light cord and how Grandpa had to fix it.

Recently, I had my office painted so everything in that room is in a different place.

"Bello …" Jeremiah chanted. "My bello." (His name for bell). He's looking on the book shelve where Grandma used to keep the bell just so the little man could make it ring. And what's this? The book case is moved as well—not good.

Color book … stickers … crayons. The blue crate that used to store these things had also been moved. The little man is not happy. He points to let me know that the blue crate belongs next to the computer stand so that he can easily access his special drawer. No crayons. No stickers and the bello is no where to be found.

"No, I do not like," J told me in no uncertain terms. I hear about this problem for a good ten minutes before he finally toddles out to the kitchen for a cookie.

I hear heartfelt sobbing.

"What's the matter? Did you hurt yourself?" He comes to Grandma for a hug.

"Too big." He cries. "Too big."

"Pa. You have to break the cookie in two, like Grandma does."

"For heaven sakes, who doesn't want a big chocolate chip cookie?" Pa wants to know.

"I little," J sobs.

I break the cookie in half and give him one for each hand, and pour some milk in his special cup. Problem solved.

J gobbles down the cookies and gives Pa "the look" before he darts out of the room to play with his toys.

"Sometimes it's the smallest decisions that can change your life forever."
~Keri Russell

Grandpa's Barn

"A little and a little, collected together, becomes a great deal; the heap
in the barn consists of single grains, and drop and drop makes an
inundation"

~Ancient Proverb

J loves to visit Grandpa's barn and what boy wouldn't find that a great adventure. You have to see Pa's barn to appreciate the excitement. (Must be a man/boy thing).

As soon as the little man comes through the door he takes off his shoes, a custom at his house, and parks them right next to Pa's. "Big shoes, little one," he chides.

He runs wild through the house to make sure all of his toys, blocks, books and cars are where they are supposed to be, especially brown bear. Brown bear better be in his chair. J is quickly learning that Gamma loves change. Once he's satisfied that everything is A-OK. He runs back to the utility room to retrieve his shoes.

"Outside, Pa."

"To the park?" Pa asks.

"No," J shakes his head, "Pa's barn ... tractors."

Off they trot out to the back forty. One of the big attractions in the barn is Pa's collection of tractors. Big ones and little ones. And J has to sit on them all and pretend to drive them, and the 4-wheeler and the motorcycle, too. His head is lost inside of Grandpa's helmet.

"Need a hat." J reminds Pa.

Then it's a mad-dash across the lawn to see the neighbor's dogs, two very large dogs and one little pup. "Puppies ... .puppies." J squeals in delight.

It's hilarious watching the dogs and the boy run up and down the fence line. I should have thought of this activity before nap. Grandma's tired. I have no idea how Pa keeps up with the little man.

Then it's on to our backyard park ... the swing set in all it's glory. J looks at me as if to say, "at least my swings are still in the same spot."

"Swing, Pa … higher." This goes on for half an hour. (He once actually fell asleep in the swing.) Two runs down the slide and a go-round on the merry-go-round and he's back in the house.

"Wrestle Gamma …"

Grandma's tired so I try to wrestle him into the bed!

J stayed with Grandpa one afternoon while I ran to do some errands. "Don't worry, Gamma, we'll be working in the barn."

"If someone is too tired to give you a smile, leave one of your own, because no one needs a smile as much as those who have none to give."
~Author unknown

Holy Mokes

"So I'm driving home last night from Saginaw and it starts to rain. Jeremiah says, "Holy mokes, Daddy, water." I laughed all the way home."

~Matthew Hawkins

"The best thing one can do when it's raining is to let it rain."

~Henry Wadsworth Longfellow

My son was helping one of my friends with a computer problem and asked me to go along to keep an eye on the little man. On the way home, the wind came up; the sky got dark … we ran smack dab into a thunder storm; the rain came down in torrents.

Suddenly, we hear a voice in the back seat. "Holy 'mokes, Dad. Water." We laughed ourselves silly.

"Jeremiah, where did you hear that?" His daddy asked.

"Gamma say it."

I guess I might have said "Holy smokes" at some point in time—not that week that I could remember but all the way home we heard, "Holy 'mokes. Water."

Be careful grownup lips what you say; little ears might be listening.

"May you always have work for your hands to do.
May your pockets hold always a coin or two.
May the sun shine bright on your window pane.
May the rainbow be certain to follow each rain.
May the hand of a friend always be near you.
And may God fill your heart with gladness to cheer you."

~Irish Blessing

Wrestling—Definitely a Boy's Sport

"I hate questioning, but I love wrestling."
~Aaron Smith

J doesn't even get in the house and he wants Grandma to wrestle with him. I'm not sure how or when this sport got started but for some reason or other, J wants to wrestle with Grandma. (And, we must have our jeans on when we wrestle).

"Grandma's old," I tell J. "Grandma can't wrestle."

"No, Gamma you not old, let's wrestle." The little man insists as he points to the floor.

At least I have him talked into wrestling on the bed, which should be a "no no" but when you're 65 the floor is a long way down.

Wrestling is a dangerous sport when you're old. Old age is a handicap and wrestling is definitely a boy's sport. And J isn't the gentlest giant when he's wrestling which includes, bouncing, jumping and tackling.

Save yourself, Grandma—make sure there are lots of pillows on the bed; you'll need the protection—at least this grandma does.

One time while wrestling, I got hit in the nose … boy was that painful. It brought tears to my eyes. We had to stop wrestling. "Jeremiah, you're too rough, Grandma is hurt."

"Gampa …" J tore out the room and ran down the hall, "Gampa … I broke Gamma!"

"Once you've wrestled, everything else in life is easy."
~Dan Gable

Grandpa I Want to Hold You

"Always make time for the tug on your pant leg. If you don't you could miss out on something really special."
~C. Hawkins

Sometimes when the adults get together a 2-year old can be over looked. Everyone was talking at once trying to get their point across, telling their story, talking about things adults talk about. No one was paying attention to Little J.

He tried to tell his story but no one listened. He sang as loud as he could but no one heard. He danced but no one saw. He loudly banged on his drum. Even that antic merited little attention.

The adults kept right on doing what they were doing.

"Dink," J shouted finally going to the refrigerator himself.

"Candy?" He asked. No one gave him a piece, not even Grandma. She was always good for candy.

"Swing me." J demanded of his Grandpa to no avail.

The adults just kept on doing what adults do.

Finally in desperation, J tugged at his Grandpa's pant leg. He kept tugging and tugging ...

"What is it little man?"

"Gampa I want to hold you."

That got our attention as Grandpa reached down and picked J up; he got the biggest squeeze ever!

Sometimes the little man just wants to be held.

"When you smiled you had my undivided attention. When you laughed you had my urge to laugh with you. When you cried you had my urge to hold you. When you said you loved me, you had my heart forever."
~Author Unknown

The Girlfriend Phone

"If The Phone Doesn't Ring, It's Me."
~Song title by Jimmy Buffet

One day Little J came to me with my old cell phone in hand and told me it was his "girlfriend phone" and proceeded to call Lana. Lana is a friends daughter, about a year or so older than J. He calls Lana often.

"Hi Lana ... wanna come over to play ... .I at Gamma's house ... see you soon. Bye bye, Lana."

These calls go on all day long several times a day. He makes the little ringing sound ... bring ... bring ... bring, answers the phone and carries on, sometimes, rather lengthy conversations. Sometimes, it's cousin Ty calling. Other times he might call my daughter's dog, Dudley. But he can only call Lana on the "girlfriend phone."

"My phone ring off the hook," J said one day out of the blue.

He's two. Where does he come up with these things?

One day we were at Pizza Hut having lunch when J's phone rang.

"It's Lana," he said. Of course it is I smiled.

Thinking this was so cute, J's mother videoed the phone call, which greatly disturbed the little man.

"No, Mama ... no," he said. He put his hands in front of her camera. He turned off his phone and turned his face away from the camera.

Some things in life are private, even when you're three, and are better left alone, especially matters of the heart.

"A girlfriend is probably the only person in this world, who understands exactly what you are saying even though you may not really be talking."
~Anonymous

Grandpa's Tractor

"I play with my tractors and live somewhat of a family life and just
try to enjoy trying to retire sooner or later."
~Dick Trickle

Grandpa collects tractors and has everything from an Alice Chalmers to
a big John Deer. J loves to go out in the pole barn just to sit on Grandpa's
tractors. When Grandpa's cutting the grass on the White, J wants to sit
there with him and drive. "I big," he informs Grandpa, "I drive."

He loves to sit high up on the John Deer as long as it isn't going any-
where, but the minute Grandpa goes to start it up, Little J is off and running.

"Don't you want a ride on Grandpa's big green tractor?" I asked.

"Nooo," he says.

"Why not?"

"I too little!"

I guess he's not quite ready to go green, yet.

"Everybody wants to help and there seems to be a job that fits what
people like to do. One of my son's friends loves tractors and has
plenty of land here to mow. There is a job for everybody."
~Dawn Kelsch

Rummage Sales

My husband is a coinsurer of rummage sales and truly believes in that old saying, "One man's junk is another man's treasure." He's passing his love of sorting through other people's junk unto Little J who loves nothing better than to go from one yard sale to another sorting through boxes and boxes of discarded toys to add to his already over flowing toy box.

I like a good sale at the local Dollar Store but Grandma hates rummaging. I prefer to wait in the car and marvel over the hidden treasures J comes back with. One day, (I was sitting in the car) when I heard a scuffle between two little boys. I cranked my head to the noise to see what was going on. J comes running down the driveway with big tears in his eyes.

"Guitar, Gamma … I want guitar." He pointed to another child.

Apparently there was an argument over who would end up owning this toy. I saw the other boy walk away. "You need to go tell Grandpa," I instructed.

J dried his tears and walked back up the drive. "Gampa," I could hear him yelling, "guitar."

Little J fared quite well that day … an Elmo guitar and another cell phone!

One more stop. Grandpa found a helicopter that really flies. Yep, you guessed it. The fought-over guitar was suddenly forgotten!

A Brother for J

"Sometimes being a brother is even better than being a superhero."
~Marc Brown

Sibling relationships and 80 percent of Americans have at least one, outlast marriages, survive the death of parents, and resurface after quarrels that would sink any friendship. They flourish in a thousand incarnations of closeness and distance, warmth, loyalty and distrust.
~Erica E. Goode, "The Secret World of Siblings," *U.S. News & World Report*, 10 January 1994

It was in July of 2011 that the announcement was made: Little J was going to have a little brother. We were all pretty excited about this news—well, most of us, anyway.

When asked if he was going to have a little brother in the near future, J replied, "No sister." He was quite certain of that fact. After all, cousin Ty had a sister and some of his friends in the toddler class at church had sisters—it made since that the new sibling at his house would most definitely be a sister named Lucy.

When we finally convinced him that he was going to be a big brother he resigned himself to the fact and decided to name his little bro Thomas after Thomas the train. Since he wasn't really into Thomas the Train, I had no idea where he came up with this idea. Although his parents blamed me for putting this notion into his head, honest, I didn't do it!

But one day, I casually asked J, what are you going to name your new brother? "Tommy," he said.

"Oh, Thomas, that's a nice name."

"No, Tommy," he said.

OK then, it's better than Thomas the Train!

Just to set the record straight ... Jacob, Jaden, John ... his parents haven't decided on a name. It could very well turn out to be Tommy. No matter what the little fellow is called, Grandma is looking forward to his arrival—it'll be nice for Little J to have someone else to wrestle with!

"It snowed last year: I made a snowman and my brother knocked it down and I knocked my brother down and then we had tea."

~Dylan Thomas

Welcome to the Family

"Siblings are the people we practice on, the people who teach us about fairness and cooperation and kindness and caring - quite often the hard way."

~Pamela Dugdale

Asher William, weighing in at a healthy 9 pounds came into the world a week later then expected on February 27th, my brother Mark's birthday. Labor was induced at 11:00 in the morning. My daughter (Aunt Heidi) and I were running errands in town, thinking we had plenty of time to make it to the hospital for Asher's arrival. We were on route when we got the call at 12:30pm that we had a new baby.

Excited to see him, and after stopping to pick up a balloon for J, we made a mad dash up to the maternity ward to meet and greet baby Asher. Although J seemed far more excited about his balloon then he was about his brother, the picture of the two boys together for the first time is a warm and touching memory. It was indeed a precious moment.

When you ask Little J, "How do you like being Asher's big brother?"

"OK," he would say. You could tell he wasn't really sure what being a big brother would mean, but he was soon to find out.

Asher: Gender male. Origin: Hebrew. Meaning: Fortunate; happy; blessed. Pronunciation: (ASH er) form of itself (Asher). In the Old Testament, Asher was the 8th son of Jacob and the second son of Zilpa, the maid of Jacob's wife Leah. He was also the founder of the Tribe of Asher.

"Gamma, can you put baby Asher somewhere … I ready to wrestle now."

"Daddy, do we have to keep this baby?"

"A friend is a brother who was once a bother."

~Author Unknown

Bringing Baby Home

"Let the little children come to me, and do not hinder them, for the kingdom of God belongs to such as these."

~From the Bible—Mark 10:14

Bringing a new baby home is both an overwhelming event as well as an exciting event. As Grandma, it was also exhausting. We took the oldest little man home with us on birth day to entertain him for a day and a half. J did not seem in any way put off by the fact that he would spend the night with Grandma and Grandpa. However, he woke up in the middle of the night congested. He hadn't been feeling well for a couple of days.

"Gamma, I all stuffy." This announcement is followed by tears. "I want Daddy," he cried.

"Daddy's at the hospital with Mama and baby Asher." I try to sooth as best I can, but the tears continued.

"Take me to the hos-ipal …" He sobbed.

I finally convinced him that I'd take him to the hospital in the morning if he still wanted to go but that now we could rock and cuddle with our blankets. He finally fell asleep in my now aching arms. I laid him on the love seat, covered him up and slept on the big couch. Morning came; he was all smiles.

We played. We laughed. We sang songs. It was around supper time that Daddy called to say they were home and ready for J's return. We packed his bag and off we went to see the new baby and welcome him home.

Nana was holding Asher when we arrived around 7pm. and immediately handed him to me.

"No, Gamma, hold me. Hold me like a baby." J commanded.

"You are getting too big to be held like a baby," I explained. But of course, I handed Asher back to Nana and held Little J like a baby. "I don't want you to hold Asher," he said. "I want you to hold me."

This behavior I knew from past experience, Heidi tried to trade her baby brother for a dog, would continue for a few days if not weeks. Grandma could handle it. After all, the biggest little man would always be my special Little J.

"A baby will make love stronger, days shorter, nights longer, bankrolls smaller, home happier, clothes shabbier, the past forgotten, and the future worth living."
~Author Unknown

Time for Daddy to go Back to Work

"A good vacation is over when you begin to yearn for your work."
~Morris Fishbein

My son is a good husband and father. He took a week off from work to help mother settle in with the new baby, who did the best "settling" of all. The first night home was rough on everyone. Well, not everyone. Little J slept through Asher's cries to be fed. Daddy spent part of the night in his reclining chair with Asher on his chest so Mommy could get some sleep.

Little J was the only one able to bounce down the hall when morning came ready to enjoy the week with Daddy, a week that went by all to fast. Before you knew it, it was time for daddy to go back to work. J wasn't all smiles about Daddy going back to work.

I love the story of Daddy going back to work after a Christmas week break.

J: (With tears in his eyes)" Daddy I don't want you to go back to work. I miss you. I miss you right now."

I'm sure this story repeated itself when Daddy went back to work after Asher's birth. At this point in time, Daddy was J's best bud. Having a new baby to contend with and then suddenly daddy wasn't there was indeed a trauma for the little man who was no longer "the little" man.

In the days that followed things changed for Jeremiah Matthew. Little J was in time out for chasing the dog, disobeying his mother, bothering his brother. Yep, having a new baby in the house would be trying for everyone.

At least once a week we stop by the house to visit with the grandchildren. There's a new baby in the house now and of course Grandma wants to hold him. That doesn't set to well with Little J who is not so patiently waiting for a turn with Grandma. It isn't easy being number two when you've been number one for three years.

J: "Gamma I want you to put baby Asher on the floor and play with me."

Grandma: "Asher is too little."

J: "I don't think he is."

J: "Gamma I want to go to your house right now."

Grandma: "But, no one is home at Grandma's house."

J: "How come?"

Grandma: "Because Grandma is at J's house."

J: "Oh … can you go home now so I can come to your house?"

J: "Mommy when can we take baby Asher back to the hospital?"

We were visiting Cousin Mimi and Uncle Dan one day. Uncle Dan asked J if he liked his little brother. "Not talking," J said ignoring any further comments about his "big brother" status.

I guess he didn't want to talk about baby Asher, at least not that day.

"Gampa can we go to the park?" Grandpa reminds J that we are watching Baby Asher so we can't go to the park. "We can just put him in his crib and go to the park," J says.

"Those are my toys. no no baby Asher," J pulls blocks from baby Asher's chubby little fists. "Here, you can play with this pillow." Toys or a pillow? Let's think about that.

And Grandma got "the look" when she was playing blanket peek-a-boo with Asher. "Gamma, that's my game with you." J looked really hurt; it's a look I'll never forget. I will figure out a new game to play with Baby Asher.

"See things from the boy's point of view."

~Robert Baden-Powell

The Rules of the Game

"We do not stop playing because we grow old. We grow old because we stop playing."

~Author Unknown

Isn't it funny … with the first baby, you can't wait for them to crawl, stand, walk and talk. And, with that first child there's sanitizer in every room; second baby comes along; you want to keep them a baby as long as possible and you can't find the sanitizer!

Jeremiah is almost three going on five! He's at that inquisitive stage of life.

J: "Gamma know what this is?"
Grandma: "Yes." I say.
J: "What is it?" J wants to know. So comes the explanations of life.
J: "Gamma know where Gampa is?"
Grandma: "Yes," I say, "He's downstairs."
J: "I go downstairs, too." He's off only to return clutching M&M's in both hands.
J: "Gamma know what these is?"
Grandma: "M&M's." I answer.
J: "Candy with nuts," he says, "for me to eat!"
J always shares with Grandma and anyone else who happens to be around.

He likes to play Yahtzee and Uno and any other game he can talk Grandma into playing. His favorite game is Wheel of Fortune.

He gets out his tools to fix broken lawn mowers and likes to measure everything including Grandma! I'm 6 inches tall, in case you're wondering. And, these days, Grandpa has to tighten his toes, using his tools, of course.

"Gamma, let's play 'blow the roof off.' Like this," J sees my raised eyebrows and proceeds to put pillows over our heads so he can blow them off.

"Stop it! Stop it!" he yells whenever a wild card comes up in Uno.

"What does stop it mean?" Should I dare ask?

"It means stop it," J explains. "Stop playing …" or rename the color whatever mood he is in that day. The rules forever change, but one thing stays the same—he's the winner, for now. We'll work on that.

New game at age 3 is the attack of the killer mosquito. He's the mosquito naturally. Can you guess who gets attacked? That would be Grandma!

"If you must play, decide upon three things at the start: the rules of
the game, the stakes, and the quitting time."
~Chinese Proverb

Wheel of Fortune

"It is in games that many men discover their paradise."
~Robert Lynd

J loves Wheel of Fortune. He's been watching it religiously since he was old enough to watch TV. His parents recorded it so he can watch it whenever he wants. Unfortunately, that is not the case at Grandma's house. Have you ever tried to explain to a little one that Grandma only gets Wheel at 7 pm, that we cannot play it at 3:00 in the afternoon! He gets pretty frustrated. "But I want to watch Wheel now, Gamma."

When he was two he took this multicolored circle magnet off the frig; it then became his "Wheel of Fortune." He carried it around for the longest time. Last Christmas I asked him what he most wanted for Christmas. "I want Wheel of Fortune," he said very matter of fact about it. When we would go shopping, we would have to go down the toy isle and look for that game. So, J and I got the game Wheel of Fortune for Christmas last year. We had to change the way you play it, you know—adapted for a three-year old. We cover all the letters. You spin the wheel, if you land on pink you get to uncover two letters. If you get a bankrupt, you don't get to uncover any letters, except, if you're Jeremiah then, of course, the rule changes and you get to uncover the curly "q."

When we play the game, J is Jeremiah Pat and I'm Grandma Vanna, and I'm also the announcer. We say: Wheel of Fortune together then I have to say, here's Jeremiah Pat or spin the wheel Jeremiah Pat. If he gets a bankrupt, I have to say, "That's darn terrible," while he makes the sound that the wheel makes when a bankrupt occurs.

The downside of this exciting game is that Jeremiah Matthew as now become Jeremiah Pat. If you asked him what's your name, he'll ultimately (most of the time) say, "My name is Jeremiah Pat." To which his parents say, "Thank you, Grandma."

"You're welcome."

136

Michael Jordon said about basketball, "Even when I'm old and grey, I won't be able to play it, but I'll still love the game." That's exactly how I feel about playing Wheel of Fortune with J. I'll always love that game.

A Three Day Week at Aunt Heidi's House

"Only an Aunt can give hugs like a mother, can keep secrets like a sister, and share love like a friend."
~Spanish Proverb

Jeremiah was excited about going to spend a couple days with Aunt Heidi and Uncle Dave. His parents had spent a lot of time preparing him for his three night four day visit.

"I'm going to play with Dudley," he was happy to announce, "and wrestle with Uncle Dave."

Dudley is Heidi's Yorkie-poo, a puppy with enough energy to keep up with J. They can spend hours chasing one another. Days before he was to leave for his big trip, J would take out his "girlfriend phone" to call Dudley and let him know he was coming.

We were all a little apprehensive as to how Little J would handle three nights away from his parents and his little brother.

But our worry seemed in vain. The first day was filled with fun things to do, like a trip to the children's museum in Ann Arbor and lunch at Zimmermen's Deli, a good place to spend a rainy day. He wanted to go back the next day!

That night his daddy called to see how he was doing. "Do you want to talk to Daddy?" Aunt Heidi asked.

"I busy," Jeremiah said matter of fact. He was playing with Dudley and eating cake.

But it warms my heart to know that when Grandma called the next day, Jeremiah was excited to tell me all about the museum, how Uncle Dave couldn't go 'cuz he wasn't feeling good. J and Aunt Heidi were baking cupcakes and walking in the woods. Did he miss us? Sadly, I don't think so. Maybe, just a little? I could hope.

Aunt Heidi even got him to take an afternoon nap, something Grandma is still working on! Hum-m, perhaps we need more walks in the woods or a good run through Grandpa's two acres!

"Grandma will see you on Wednesday for lunch ..."

"No, Gamma I stay with Aunt Heidi and go to the museum and wrestle with Dudley ... bye bye Gamma ..."

I tearfully hung up. I miss you Little J. My little man is growing up.

"Aunts usually are very important part of our lives. They are the ones we usually grow with us, and have always been there to listen to us."

~Author unknown

All Boy

Matt Hawkins on Facebook

"So, Easter Sunday Jeremiah got a new T ball set (from his Aunt Heidi) to start working on his baseball skills. We were at Grandma's and Grandpa's outside happily playing when the dog found a baby bunny. Jeremiah came up with his bat and says, 'Daddy I want to hit it with my bat.' when I told him that wasn't OK, he seemed so disappointed. He's such a boy."

Easter 2012, an Easter I won't soon forget. May I take the liberty to add to my son's blurb? Of course I can, I'm the author of this book.

It was a busy Easter … church service, egg hunts, Easter baskets, and a nice dinner with family and time to play outdoors, batting balls and chasing dogs.

Why did the dogs (Wendell and Dudley) have to find bunnies on Easter of all days? Especially since on our way home from church, Jeremiah decided he would look for the Easter bunny—not that he had an inkling of what or who that is. We found no bunnies until later in the day when Dudley found a nest with two baby bunnies in it. "Why Easter, Dudley?"

Picture this: Dudley is running through the yard with a baby bunny in his mouth. (Aunt Heidi says it was a baby mouse.) Wendell is chasing Dudley. Aunt Heidi is chasing both dogs, yelling at Dudley to "drop it." J is bringing up the rear …

"No Easter bunny," J is screaming at Dudley. It was a wild scene indeed. "Let's hope it's not a bunny on Easter of all days," I say to myself.

One bunny down and the other in a very weak condition, would he make it? Not if J had his way … thus the entry on Facebook the following day.

Sometimes, a bunny just doesn't make it—for whatever reason.

"Weak is the joy which is never wearied."
~William Blake

Shopping

"The quickest way to know a woman is to go shopping with her."
~Marcelene Cox

J comes to visit every other Friday while Mom goes grocery shopping. He's so excited that he doesn't have time to take off his coat. He goes immediately to the toy box, and dumps all the toys out. Then it's onto the stuffed animals; he rearranges those and makes sure they are sitting the way he wants them. He sits brown bear in the rocking chair and rocks him momentarily, listens to praying bear recite "Now I lay me down to sleep ..." he especially likes the "Amen" part. Then he hauls out his riding car and his lawn mower. Without fail whenever he visits, he has to fix the lawn-mowers so he can mow the carpet!

This habit of watching J while his mother goes grocery shopping is the best habit I have to date. It gives Mom some me-time and gives Grandma some J time and eventually, when he's a little older, some Asher time as well.

Asher was just about a month old when Mom dropped J off at Grandma's for some shopping time.

"Don't forget Asher," J yelled as Mom was getting ready to go! He pointed toward the front door.

Guess he wanted to make sure that she knew Asher wasn't staying.

Jeremiah likes to pretend he's going shopping in his pink and purple car with play money in hand.

"Where you going to shop?" I asked.

"How 'bout K-Mart." Off he goes down the hall. A man after my own heart. Or he likes to get out the shoe house and have the Webble people who live there go shopping in the Webble bus.

Sometimes, he and I and Grandpa actually go shopping and of course, Grandma always buys him some little trinket or treats. I know this is not a good habit to get into but grandchildren are spoiled when they come to Grandma's house as I'm sure they are at Nana's house as well. If you're a grandma, you know what I'm talking about. Of course, when we are shopping we have to stop at a rummage sale–oh the treasures the two of them, Grandpa and J, find. And of course, J is always ready to go to McDonald's or Taco Bell for lunch!

One visit he was whining because I wouldn't buy him a Happy Meal (he wanted the toy). "You already have those toys," I told him.

"I want to buy it for Baby Asher," he said. "He will like it."

Interesting, especially since Baby Asher is only three months old and isn't into eating happy meals.

"I love shopping, especially food shopping."
~Emma Bunton

Poo Poo or Poop Poo

"The most important part of education is proper training in the nursery."
~Plato

I hope my son won't be too disgruntled with me if I tell this year's (2012) Father's Day story. We were supposed to go on a park picnic but rain kept us indoors so I took the family out for steak. J was too busy running around the table to eat (with exception of some peanuts and a nice warm buttered bread roll). Just before our meals arrived, he loudly announced, "Dad, I have to go poop—right now."

Have you ever noticed during the potty training stage of life you can't get them to go to the bathroom at home, they're either too busy or they simply forget, but take them out to a restaurant and they have to go every time.

So off to the bathroom Daddy and son went. They were gone an awfully long time. When they finally returned, Daddy was red-faced.

"Next time," he told Mommy, "you're taking him to the bathroom."

"Why, what happened?" We all wanted to know. We shouldn't have asked.

"Poo poo talk … too many questions about poop … why do people have to poop, look how big my poop is … what does your poop look like … it was embarrassing," Daddy said. (We were trying to control our laughter.)

"It was the potty room," J was all smiles.

Well, what is one supposed to talk about in the bathroom? We were glad when our food arrived but for the most part our appetites were lost.

Anyone for dessert?

"A child can go only so far in life without potty training. It is not mere coincidence that six of the last seven presidents were potty trained, not to mention nearly half of the nation's state legislators."
~Dave Barry

Out of the Mouths of Babes

Other parents and grandparents share:
We've all shared amusing stories, questions or remarks from our children and/or grandchildren from time to time; some of us more than others. I admit, I have gone overboard a time or do when it comes to my grandchildren, but honest, I'm seen them do and say things I couldn't possibly have made up—I'm sure you have, too!

The funny things kids say and do sure keep us on our toes. They make us laugh and sometimes they make us cry, but mostly they give us "food for thought" or in my case, material for my book!

Thank you to all those friends and relatives who shared their stories. I couldn't have done this last chapter of "Touching Grandma's Heart" without you. I hope some of the stories in this book have truly touched your heart. And for those of you whom I have bored to tears with stories of my adorable grandchildren, I apologize, but it doesn't mean I'm going to stop with the stories anytime soon. After all, grandson number two has arrived. I'm already thinking of a squeal to this book, "Awesome Asher"—good title, don't you agree? And now, enjoy stories, out of the mouths of babes, from other parents and grandparents.

A Grandma from Michigan
I was visiting my five-year old grandson and found him lying on his bed, hands tucked behind his head, in deep thought.

"Grandson, what are you doing?" I asked.

"I'm having a life change," he said.

Jill Place – Michigan
I gave Tyler his summer hair cut tonight. He saw it and immediately started sobbing, "Mommy, no, no, no. I don't like it. I want someting deeeferent. Mommy. You made me so sad!! I look like a bad guy!" Now I know that Tyler doesn't like short hair.

Helen Sanborn – Ohio

Paisley throws a tantrum when we tell her "No" or "Don't chew on Daddy's iPhone" or "No pulling sister's hair" and apparently has heard the word "no" so many times that she is now saying, "Mama, no!" Isn't this sass a little early for 9 months?

Helen Sanborn – Ohio

I explained to Lily about fasting tonight and how kids can find ways to participate. She ruminated for a minute, then, said, "I've decided I choose ice cream, not a fast."

From a Michigan Auntie

My niece decided to try out her mother's new scissors by giving the cat a hair cut!

That's nothing; my nephew used my chap stick on the cat's butt and then put it back in my drawer!

Helen Sanborn – Ohio

Our family went to the zoo today and Lily saw a man with a blue Mohawk with his kids and said excitedly (and loudly), "Dad, look at that guy! He looks like a peacock!!" These chats about manners just keep happening.

Dan – Indiana

I asked my grandson what he wanted for lunch.

"Pizza, ice cream and candlelopes!" he answered

Helen Sanborn – Ohio (More from Lily)

Lily wanted to wear a dress yesterday that she had outgrown and was too short. When we told her she needed to choose another dress, she stomped her foot, shook her head, and said, "That's it... I QUIT!!" and proceeded to give herself a time out in her bedroom.

Lily saying the fruits of the Spirit this morning: "Love, joy, peace, patience, gentlemen..." Haha!!

This is what happens when Lily goes to Target with just Daddy and no Mama. She picked out matching Easter dresses for her and Paisley, complete with bunny slippers and a sparkly bunny mask.

We don't know where they get this stuff. But somehow they manage to make us laugh, even though we're sometimes horrified about the things they say or do that we didn't teach them.

Jon Gittins – Bay City
Ethan: We have to eat our food before we play, right? Because if I were you, I would tell me that too. (From the mind of a four year old.)

Ann Haskins – Midland
I was in my bathroom when my 5 year old grand daughter came in, seeing me take my upper denture out her eyes got as large a saucers, she asked grandma how did you do that? She then called for her sister saying come here Grandma can take her teeth out. They were both amazed. We laughed together when I explained.

Julie Gittins – Bay City
I told my grandson we were going to go through the "drive through" for supper. "But I don't want to go through the drive through. I would to go to the in-drive."

From the Internet
Funny Things Kids Say and Do – those Hilarious, sometimes shocking things we didn't teach them – by Apryl Ducan

You can probably relate to these scenarios of the child who:
- screams when she sees a ladybug but has no problem bringing you a roach by the legs.
- updates your Facebook status with every letter on the keyboard.
- calls Mommy's feminine hygiene products, "really big bandages."
- dumps cornmeal all over the kitchen floor to pretend she's on a sandy beach.
- wears your nice oven mitts on her feet.

146

- mispronounces Wal-Mart as Mal-Wart.
- puts cat stickers on the dog and dog stickers on the cat.
- prays for her grandparents, friends and the playground.
- asks you to take her to the baby store so she can trade her new baby brother for a sister.
- uses Mommy's bra as a protective shield from brain-sucking aliens.
- says she got a poo poo when she means a boo boo.

Thanks for buying my book. I hope you enjoyed reading it as much as I enjoyed writing it. And thanks to Little J for all those wonderful delightful stories and expressions. I know there's more to come and I'm looking forward to them!

~*Connie*

Acknowledgements:

Quotes from:

The Quote Garden celebrating 14+ years online. a harvest of quotations for the word lover. quotegarden.com 1998-2012 A personal collection of favorite quotes and sayings, inspirational, funny, thought-provoking, motivational, famous, literary. This free, searchable and ever growing website is visited daily by writers, speakers, students and word searches. www.quotegarden.com/children

Famous quotes and authors.com: (The quotes on this website are the property of their respective authors.) Information has been reproduced for informational and educational purposes. 2011

The Book of Unusual Quotations – Harper and Row Publishers, 1957. New York, Evanston and London.

Brainy Quote – Online www.brainyquotes.com; Book Rags Media Network

Apryl Duncan – Stay-at-Home Moms Guide

The Quotation Page – Quotes of the Day: quotationpage.com & Michael Moncur 1994-2012; www.quotegarden.com/children

Inspirational Quotes – Ask.com www.inspirationa-quotesinfo (Public domain)

The Holy Bible – New American Standard - Thomas Nelson Publisher, 1985, 1978 (Scriptures used by permission)
Famous Quotes and More – online: www.famousquotes.com

Apples of Gold - compiled by Jo Petty published by C.R. Gibson Co
Quotes of Wisdom: A select collection of quotes of wisdom by Simran Khurana - about.com/guided (Professor Khurana uses the wisdom in quotations to electrify her classes)

Children's Dreams – Jonathan Malory: www.meaningofdreams.org/ dream/themes/children's dreams.htm

www.ingramcontent.com/pod-product-compliance
Lightning Source LLC
Chambersburg PA
CBHW030105070426
42448CB00037B/978

* 9 7 8 1 6 0 9 2 0 0 6 6 4 *